Best wishes

CW00326352

Eat Like a Horse, Drink Like a Fish ...

Also by Tom O'Connor and published by Robson Books

From the Wood to the Tees
The World's Worst Jokes
One Flew Over the Clubhouse
Take a Funny Turn
Follow Me, I'm Right Behind You!

Eat Like a Horse, Drink Like a Fish ...

A Bellyful of Laughter

Tom O'Connor

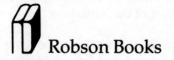

Robson Books

First published in Great Britain in 1996 by Robson Books Ltd, Bolsover House, 5–6 Clipstone Street, London W1P 8LE

Copyright © 1996 Tom O'Connor

The right of Tom O'Connor to be identified as author of this work has been asserted by him in accordance with the Copyright, Designs and Patents Act 1988

Illustrated by Jim Hutchings

British Library Cataloguing in Publication Data
A catalogue record for this title is available from the British Library

ISBN 1 86105 068 2

All rights reserved. No part of this publication may be reproduced, stored in a retrieval system, or transmitted in any form or by any means, electronic, mechanical, photocopying, recording or otherwise, without the prior permission in writing of the publishers.

Photoset in North Wales by Derek Doyle & Associates, Mold, Flintshire. Printed and bound in Great Britain by Butler & Tanner Ltd, Frome and London

For Patricia Jade. You are as lovely as your mother and, like her, you follow the music.

Contents

1

Nothing Holds Liquor
Better than a Bottle

I suppose in all the world it would be hard to find a place to compare with a typical British pub. The home of some of the most peculiar and interesting characters you'd ever want to meet. Pubs on Friday and Saturday nights are full of people you couldn't invent. They must live in the places because you never see them in the street do you? I love the descriptions given of inveterate boozers:

'Wears square-toed shoes so he can get nearer the bar.'
'Suffers from lumbago of the right hip. It comes from putting wet change in your back pocket.'
'Love makes the world go round but whisky's cheaper and more reliable.'

It seems, in our fantasies, that we all love a drunk, preferably if he's not boring us to death at the bar, fighting, or causing general mayhem. The trouble is that alcohol is a good friend but a bad enemy. A little like water really. A little is fine, but a torrent can be lethal. So when we look at the world of the imbiber, let us look realistically at the fun that drink can arouse, without forgetting the very obvious pitfalls that there are along the way. Remember little adages like:

'By drinking everyone else's health he ruined his own!'

'Show me a man who can eat, drink and be merry and I'll show you a fat, grinning drunk!'

When my own personal diet was in operation and I was trying hard to lose weight, give up smoking and get fit, the major obstacles were pubs and clubs. Not because they are bad places. In fact quite the opposite. The friendliness, atmosphere and general buzz of a bar makes me its greatest fan. No, my problem was that that very same *bon accord* and all-round good fun was tempting me to relax. And once the brain relaxes of course, so does the will. Suddenly the cravings come upon you:

'Just one pint and maybe a small cigar.'

'Maybe just another half and a couple of pickled eggs.'

It really is hard to resist that little voice behind the right temple, but it can be done by throwing oneself wholeheartedly into the pub entertainment. Luckily these days hostelries sell meals and coffee. And, with the dangers of drink-driving firmly in mind, people will quite happily leave a coffee drinker to his own devices and not pound him into having 'just a wee dram'. Thank God, say I, and nice to see common sense prevailing at long last. So, armed with a pot of coffee, and no urge to murder the pickled eggs, it's possible to sink peacefully into the life and activities of the local and wind down after a long day.

Fruit machines, space invaders, juke boxes, pool, skittles, karaoke, you name it and the pubs have got it. Satellite TV, golf simulators, live entertainers, on and on goes the list. Something for everyone, and all in comfort and safety. Barflies with tons of advice on any or all subjects. People who've been there, done that, seen them, and are prepared to share their experiences. Men selling dodgy watches, ladies selling roses, lovers telling lies, lovers' partners believing every word. All are there and all are open to view. Let's take a look at a few, but I'd like to begin with that supreme pub sporting event. No, not darts, not cards, not dominoes (although I do like that tale about the old chap who was so tight fisted that when he played dominoes he wouldn't knock in case the waiter brought another round of drinks). No, none of the above. *The* event of all events has to be the pub quiz. Surely the one moment of every week when the brains of the bar room show their skill, their powers of memory and their coolness under pressure. Why, it's a little like *Mastermind*, but more life and death if you know what I mean.

My first introduction into this academic world was made through a Liverpool pal of mine called Roy. Roy was a drinker. The legend was he could swallow anything except the fact that America won the Second World War. Guinness and port wine was his favourite tipple although the story goes that he once got so desperate he took to drinking Windolene window cleaner. 'Terrible hangovers but beautifully clear eyes,' his brother said. Roy was a quiz league referee and would take me to various competition nights. Believe me, if you think the FA Cup Final is a cauldron of pressure, you should try the Jaw Bone pub on a Friday night. These 'dos' generally start with a little friendly banter.

'Now then, Roy,' said one team member at the Park Hotel, 'no hard questions, OK?'

'Listen,' said Roy, 'there's no such thing as a hard question, because when you know the answers they're all easy' – sensible.

What surprised me most was the *level* of questions being asked. As a TV quiz host there is a tendency to forget that, whilst I have to push a show along with a fairly comfortable set of questions, there's no such restriction when live in a bar. Ten million viewers don't want to watch a programme where most of the answers given are wrong – not good TV – sounds of 'click' would be heard as the nation changed channels. But live in the lounge of the local, the assembled host couldn't give a toss if only one question was answered correctly all night – so long as their team answered it.

Who played in goal for Everton in the 1933 Cup Final?
Who was Hitler's number two?
What is the height of Mount Everest?
Name seven EEC countries.
What was the highest, lowest, longest, shortest, quickest, slowest, oldest, youngest ...

The questions just roll on and surprisingly the answers come bouncing back – more right than wrong.

But, I've got to say, my all-time favourites have got to be the trick questions, or the daft ones. You know the type? 'In the song "Sylvia's Mother" what was the daughter's name?' Think about it.

'Who was the only jockey since the war to ride in the

Grand National, fall at the first fence, remount the horse and go on to win the race?' asked Roy, only to be greeted with silence and empty stares.

'Give up?' he asked.

'Yes,' they all mumbled.

'It was George Formby in the film *Come on George*.'

That caused an outcry so loud it beat the reaction given to this sporting gem: 'Boxing,' said my mate. 'Here are four well-known names – Joe Louis, Rocky Marciano, Muhammad Ali, Sugar Ray Robinson.'

'All world champions and all American,' offered one team member.

'Agreed,' said Roy, 'but who was the first one to wear white gloves?'

Silence.

'Stumped?' asked Mr Quizmaster. 'Al Jolson,' he said, and ducked just as the beer mats showered around him.

Still, a little fun breaks the monotony sometimes and fun is the business of any pub or club these days. No matter where we stray on these fair shores, there's always a local where a person can unwind and have a chat with genial strangers who rapidly become friends. It must be such a blessing for those people from other countries who find themselves in new surroundings and long for the chance to integrate. Take the case of the Japanese businessman freshly appointed to a major company in Britain and posted to the West Country. Here he found a beautiful old cottage to rent in a dreamy little Devon village. On the first night he decided to pop into The Ferret to try to get the feel of his new surroundings. Bidding a fond farewell to his good lady, and promising not to be long (famous last words) he toddled off. Several hours later he returned in very bad repair and walking in that familiar gait of the toper – three paces forward, two back and one to the side.

'Well?' inquired the worried, but now relieved missus, 'where have you been till this time?' (Oh, how those words ring familiar.)

'You won't believe it,' said the grinning one. (Here comes another classic excuse.) 'I went into the Ferret place and the men were drinking large glasses of what looked like yellow tea, so I ordered the same. The manager told me they were pints of beer, bitter I think it is called. I got to chat to some people at the bar and they were very friendly. They bought me drinks, I bought them drinks. My, my, I've never seen such thirsts. In one corner of the room some men were playing a game and asked me if I would like to join in.'

'And did you?' asked the intrigued wife.

'Yes', he said, 'and it was great fun. On the wall was a round board full of numbers. The men were taking turns to throw little arrows at the board and make them stick. I took my turn and threw the arrows where I was told. My team kept winning and the others kept buying me pints. Pint, pint, pint – I don't know how many I drank.'

'And what, may I ask,' said the good lady, 'was the name of this arrows game?'

'I think,' said her husband, 'it was called Jammy Jap Swine…'

Ah, the joys of the inebriated. Isn't that old saying so true – 'Where there's no sense there's no feeling.'

Some of the funniest drinking places I know are wine lodges. For those who are unfamiliar with them let me explain. The basic set-up is as a pub, but the main drinks are wines from all over the world – particularly from Australia. The drinks are great value for money, good taste and not a little kick on occasions. The problem arises, of course, as with all spirits and wines, when the drinker totally relaxes into the surrounding

atmosphere and begins quaffing shorts at the same rate at which he drinks beer. This is what's known as entering the fast lane and can only lead to tears. But on the way tears of laughter can be shed by those who witness the proceedings. I heard a great story from a Liverpool taxi driver about a fare he had to pick up.

'Go to Yates's Wine Lodge in Moorfields and pick up a gentleman called Casey. Could be the worse for wear,' said the voice on the radio. Round sped the cab and there, swaying ominously on the steps of Yates's was the fare.

'Taxi for Casey?' shouted the driver.

'Th'ash me, th'ash me,' slurred the customer – a man who'd just been introduced to a new brew called the Back to School Drink – two glasses and you are in a class of your own.

'Jump in,' said the cabbie, although to be fair, jumping was much too difficult for this man who had trouble even walking. In eventually slumped the bullet-proof one.

'Where to?' asked the driver.

'Yates's Wine Lodge, Moorfields,' said the drunk and fell asleep.

What to do? I mean *what* to do? How do you tell this guy he's already there? More importantly, how do you wake him up to tell him? Suddenly – ping! – an idea formed and the cabbie just sat back and waited three minutes. Then, he eased off the handbrake, rolled forward a couple of yards and banged on the brakes.

'All right mate,' he shouted, 'we're here – Yates's.'

'Wah? Wah? Oh! How much is that?' asked the newly roused one.

'Call it two fifty for cash, friend,' smiled the driver.

'Here's three,' said the wino, 'and next time don't go so fast' and fell out of the taxi.

What a tale, what a teller. Probably the most underrated breed of folk in the world are the men and women of the taxi service. Always a gag, always a witty remark, always an opinion on world affairs. I love them and I collect their anecdotes. I figure that for every five or six you've heard there'll be at least one good one that you haven't. Take the Dublin cabbie who was funny by accident whilst telling me a tale of woe.

'You're not the only famous person I've picked up you know,' he began.

'No?'

'Indeed not. I once had the great pleasure of driving Mr Dave Allen, that fine Irish comedian,' said O'Malley (for such was his name) proudly.

'Is that so?' said I. 'I've never met the man but I greatly admire him and I'll bet he's a very nice fellow as well.'

'Well, you see, there's the point,' O'Malley mused, 'I'm not too sure.'

'Why not?' I pressed.

'Well, you see,' went on the driver, 'he sat in the back, told me where he was headed and before I could bid him time of day he said, "Before we start, you don't tell me any Irish jokes and I won't tell you how to drive this cab, all right?" and do you know that's all he said the whole journey.'

I calmed the fellow down by stressing that at least the encounter gave him something to talk about. As did my chat with a Liverpool cabbie about five years ago. Jumping into the back of the cab I immediately began to babble on about how well the city was doing and how the gloom of recession was beginning to disperse.

'Not yet,' he said over his shoulder, and out of the corner of his mouth.

'You reckon?' I said.

'I know,' he replied. 'This town is still in a bad way. In fact I'll tell you how bad a state Liverpool is in – it's eight months since somebody's been sick in the back of this cab…'

What a yardstick. I think I know what he means, but maybe the drinkers are going home by bus now, or walking, or … well, who knows. I do know that one of the funniest alcohol-related stories has been in my act off and on for over twenty years. For sure it is not true, but somewhere down the line at least parts of it have been gleaned from real life. Our tale begins with the summer holidays in the late fifties/early sixties when all of Liverpool seemed to descend upon the Isle of Man just for a day out 'like Yorkshire wakes but overseas' as my mother used to say, God bless her. In those days the main travel was by ferry and these left Liverpool at frequent intervals. In fact the most popular time to travel seemed to be about 8 am. Firstly it gave people virtually all day to enjoy the island, secondly, and most importantly, the bar on the ship was open all through the voyage. Imagine all the young buckos, myself included, drinking for three hours on the high seas – well, all right, the Irish Sea. Our favourite beverage in my teenage days was pints of Guinness and cider mixed – black velvet or, more exactly, the oblivion express. By the time we landed in Douglas we didn't know if we were on this earth or Fullers. And then, surprise, surprise, the pubs on the island were open all day – well, hold me back.

Although the strength of youth can withstand enormous quantities of liquor there does come a time when sense goes out and nonsense comes in. Just about that time the hooter would go at the docks and the message would go out, 'Get the Scousers off the island.' Many a callow youth would be dragged protesting between two policemen. 'Mind the coat pal, mind the coat' was the general protest give or take the odd expletive. Always and ever there would be a straggler to be found sitting in a gutter, head in hands. A crowd of youths asked him what was wrong.

'They've all left me.'

'Who?' they inquired.

'All of them,' he jabbered.

'Where are you from pal?'

'Liverpool.'

'Then you're with us,' said the spokesman and swiftly they scooped him up and bustled him on to the ferry. Into the bar for three hours, into a taxi at Liverpool, and all the way back to his house. There, they knocked at the door, rang the bell incessantly, shouted through the letter box and threw coins at upstairs windows. Nothing. Eventually a neighbour came out and said, 'Listen lads, you'll get no answer there. They've all gone to the Isle of Man for a fortnight...'

My thanks to the ferryman who first gave me that story. My thanks to all ferrymen and women who have made me laugh over the years. In your honour I think there should be a ninth beatitude: 'Blessed are they who ferry the seas for they shall be called the ticklers of funny bones.'

You wouldn't believe some of the true-life happenings that I've gathered from pages of ferry history. Take the case of the Irish drunks going from Dublin to Liverpool for Aintree Races during Grand National week. Synchronized drinking teams from all over Erin's Isle converging on the Stena *Hibernia* to start the journey. Feeling no pain and walking with their heads back so they wouldn't spill any, they began to climb the gang plank. All except one misguided yolk who had proceeded to the gangway which was reserved for ferry staff only – security being what it is these days.

'Hey,' bellowed an officer from the top deck. 'Get off that gangway.'

'Wha?' yelled the drunk at nobody in particular, unable to see the man on high through his alcoholic haze.

'Get off that gangway immediately,' repeated the seaman, 'that's for crew only.'

'Well, which one is for Holyhead?' asked the inebriate.

Somehow you know how he feels don't you? An invisible presence giving orders and the head not quite being able to cope. But then isn't that what's special about drink – eventually it drives out all reason and the brain goes into neutral while the body freewheels. And as if drink were not a bad enough influence, surely nothing can compete with the damage done by *free* drink. Be it the opening of a new pub, the launch of a new brew, a wedding, a funeral, a birth or a retirement, it seems as if we mortals have a small brain cell that just cannot resist the offer of 'as much as you like'. This was certainly the case with my lovely wife Pat a few years ago when the beauty of Madeira took over from the nous of Yorkshire. We'd decided to have a short break away from the children and, being just a little well known from club work, I managed to wangle a free cruise to the Canary Islands in exchange for three nights' cabaret aboard ship. Pat loves the sun, and spent most days in bikini-clad splendour on the decks chatting to other passengers. Quickly she struck up a friendship with a lovely lady, recently widowed, who'd brought her teenaged daughters on a trip to help them come to terms with their shattering loss. All went well until Madeira and the famous wine-tasting incident. As you may or may not know, there is an art to tasting wine and it seems to consist of taking a mouthful, swilling it round the tonsils and spitting it out. With Pat and her new-found friend this worked for about three sips and then they started to swallow ever such a little bit each time. Very shortly they were totally immune to the difference in tastes and were actually guzzling the stuff.

'Two more glasses of number seven,' they called to the over-worked steward, and then burst into fits of giggles. This went on for quite a while.

'I think it's good to have the occasional drink. It helps you to unwind,' said one.

Within ten minutes they had unwound so much that they couldn't stand up and a couple of crewmen and myself had to manhandle them back aboard, and down to our cabin. There they flopped face down on a bunk apiece, still clad in coats, shoes, all their clothes and clutching handbags. There they lay all that day, all that evening and the following twenty-four hours. Funny to imagine but very disconcerting for me. Where to sleep? Not the lady's cabin, it contained two teenaged girls. Not any other cabin, the ship was a sell-out. Answer? The disco. Two nights running I sat up in that place of sweat-covered walls and mega-decibel noise until every party-goer had left for bed and then I collapsed on one of the bench seats. At long last the two ladies surfaced from their comas and rejoined the human race. No mention was ever made of their two-day state. No questions were asked of anyone else's welfare and, until this moment, I've never been brave enough to tell anybody about it, although once or twice in a crowded pub I've shouted to an invisible barman, 'Two more glasses of number seven.'

I'm sure when reading these pages you will be

prompted to remember funny stories that have happened to you, or friends, or to people in your presence. Generally speaking, this sort of thing acts as a spur to remembering other stories, and so it goes on. Haven't you ever sat in company and traded anecdotes as the topics unfold? So many, so funny, and some, surely, at least eighty per cent true.

There's the one about the old codger of eighty-five who went up to the bar and asked for a pint of 1934 mild. The young assistant tried to reason with him but to no avail.

'I want a pint of 1934 mild please young man,' he insisted.

Presently the manager called the barman aside and said, 'Look he's probably doting. He doesn't know what he's saying. Just give him a pint of ordinary mild and tell him it's what he wants.'

Drink duly poured, the young man placed the glass on the bar and said, 'Here you are Granddad, here's your 1934 mild.'

'Thanks son,' beamed the old 'un, 'and here's your two pence.'

Or then there was the tale of the Salvation Army girl going round the bar with a collection box. On reaching the same old chap she asked, 'Can you spare ten pence for God?'

'How old are you?' asked the veteran.

'Eighteen,' replied the lass.

'Well I'm eighty-five,' he said. 'I'll see God before you will – I'll pay him myself.'

Or then there was the heavy drinker who picked up the wrong can and, instead of drinking beer he drank heavy-duty varnish – a terrible death, but a beautiful finish.

Or there was the distillery worker who drowned in a

vat of whisky.

'How terrible. What an awful way to go,' said a grieving relative.

'I'm not so sure,' spake his all-knowing widow. 'Apparently he got out three times to go to the loo…'

Or there were the two adventurers, lost in the Sahara Desert, who suddenly found they had run out of food and water. All they had to consume was a case of whisky. This duly done they sat drunkenly and began to work out a survival plan.

'I'll stay here and draw some SOS letters in the sand to attract passing planes. You go off and forage for food,' said one.

'Agreed,' said the slightly drunker other one, and off he set. Two hours later he returned in what appeared to be triumph.

'I've got good news and bad news,' he reported. 'The bad news is, all I could find to eat was camel dung.'

'My God,' said his now sobering partner. 'What's the good news?'

'Well,' smiled the forager, 'I've found tons of it.'

There's no end to the lunatic reasoning that drink can bring on. We've all heard of eccentric behaviour and just taken it in our stride. Admittedly, it's usually not as outrageous as the two pals who went hunting and packed quite a load of booze on the pick-up. After a heavyish liquid lunch they went into the forest and many shotgun rounds pealed out. A little while later a fellow hunter, lying still in wait for his prey, was disturbed by grunts, groans and abusive language. Rising from his hide he spotted the two trying to push the carcass of a deer through the undergrowth.

'What's going on?' he hissed.

'Just taking this back to load on the pick-up,' replied one.

'But you're using up too much energy trying to push the thing. You should pull it by the horns,' explained the disturbed hunter.

'We've tried that,' said the drunk, 'but the truck was getting further away...'

Hey ho, say you, 'twould only happen in joke or daydream. But not always so. On the most reliable authority, let me quote a story that really did occur in a Crown court not a million leagues from London Town. In the dock stood the ultimate alcoholic wreck, reduced to straining Brasso through a cloth to provide comfort for his craving, and drinking the dregs of anything medicinal or methylated in his desire to reach the painless state of the inebriate. He stood forlornly as the judge pronounced sentence. And here the twist comes into the tale. For it's not the drunk who provides the nuttiness, but the man whose profession is supposedly renowned for sobriety.

'I see,' said his honour, 'that this is your ninety-eighth conviction for drunk and disorderly behaviour. But I have decided to give you one last chance. First though, you must promise not to have another drink – not even a sherry before lunch.' I mean who is potty in this story?

More accurate, I think, is the tale of a similar drunk who, when arraigned and brought before the court was accused of being drunk and incapable.

'Not so, your honour,' he pleaded, 'I was not drunk, I was merely ill.'

'Ill?' inquired the judge, 'and what made you ill?'

'Well, sir,' explained the accused, 'I was drinking a mixture of meths and milk and I think the milk was off.' Ah! that's much more likely a tale.

But to conclude our look at drink and all its pitfalls and pleasures, why don't we have a truly classic story. I

first heard this particular anecdote in Great Yarmouth in 1977 and despite all other variations, I prefer to believe it genuinely did happen to the husband of the lady who told it to me.

Before we begin the saga, it is necessary to explain that Great Yarmouth is a beautiful spot on the east coast of Britain which, in the summer, is a holidaymaker's paradise. In winter though, we must remember that the North Sea can be a treacherous beast, and waves can be of the very large and very strong variety. So, with this in mind, let's follow the lady's husband Ken and his three pals as they go for a drink in their local one Christmas Eve lunchtime. One jar, as it does, naturally follows another as the festive spirit takes hold. Three o'clock is replaced by four-thirty in that awful whirlwind when the clock hands suddenly leap ahead without anyone noticing and then, according to an eventually sobered-up Ken, this takes place:

'We'd all decided to sup up and get home in good order (dubious behaviour for a start) when Percy suggested (always someone else is the instigator) we get a boat and go deep-sea fishing.' Whatever possessed him to think such thoughts? So the five merrymakers boarded an eight-foot boat and set out to face the North Sea. About a mile out, and still laden down with copious quantities of ale, the said Ken began to feel just a little unwell. Leaning over the side to be sick, he opened his mouth and his false teeth fell into the North Sea. Ken immediately proceeded to voice lines like, 'How very unfortunate' and 'Whatever shall I do?'

Whereupon Percy (the instigator) saw the makings of a joke to play. So taking out his own false teeth he tied them to his fishing line and said, 'You're all right Ken, I've got them.'

Seeing the gnashers, Ken grabbed them, took one look and said, 'They're not mine' and threw them into the sea as well.

Could be true, *should* be true. But we'll never know how they managed, toothless over Christmas.

2

Why Think Thin?

There's a joke in common usage which refers to a lady's fortieth birthday celebrations. The husband asked her what she would most like as a present if she had the choice.

'Of all the things in the world, I'd like to be twelve again,' she sighed.

On the evening of her special day, hubby arrived home with a box. 'Your present's inside,' he beamed, 'open it up.'

Undoing the wrapping paper and cutting through the miles of sticky tape she eventually came to a school uniform, gymslip, socks, trainers, as well as a packet of lollipops and tickets for *Babes in the Wood* on ice.

As the full meaning of the gift began to dawn, she glowered at her husband and said, 'I meant *size* twelve you moron!'

Now, there's a story that could almost be true, – well, couldn't it? Isn't it so that of all the things in the world, and it is full of many wonders, the average person with the power to choose, would choose a lean and athletic figure? Be honest. There aren't many of us who would seriously prefer to be totally unfit, flabby and generally out of condition. It's just the blooming effort of getting to be lean and athletic that is the stumbling block. But why?

Before we launch into the pros and cons of diet, exercise and such, let us determine why it is essential for us to have a specific shape.

Who, in the first place, decided that men should have mighty muscles, stomachs like washboards, acres of thick-flowing hair and a deep Mediterranean tan? Probably the same person who insisted that women have perfect hourglass figures, long, lithe legs, no cellulite and a deep Mediterranean tan. But who is to say this unknown person is right? Who is to go against all that history tells us? Take a look at paintings and sculptures going back to Roman times and before. Do you see even one that looks like what the ideal person should resemble? No. And do you know why? No such person ever existed, except in the minds of the fitness and diet freaks. OK, so there's the Mr Universe type with massive biceps, triceps, quadriceps and other 'ceps', but so what? Ever seen one of them trying to climb stairs? Ever seen one sitting comfortably in a seat on an aeroplane? And what about the ladies? Seen those wafer-thin models – do they look fit and healthy? Tell the truth. Surely if it were natural for our womenfolk to look like that, there'd be no such thing as a thriving fashion industry selling bras, tights, long dresses, short dresses and such. No, before we move on, let's all be clear about one thing – given the choice, we'd all prefer to eat what we liked, rest rather than exercise and it would be heaven if we could do it without putting on an ounce of fat.

But it's never going to be like that. So let's look at the

various ways we mere mortals try to compromise between fitness and flab. Just recently we bought a treadmill so that Pat and I can run off calories indoors out of the elements and away from eyes that could laugh at our puny efforts. This machine was in response to a genuine grumble from my good lady.

'Do you know, in the years since I had our fourth baby, I've been on diet after diet. I've just worked out that in all that time, I've lost over 1,600 lbs.'

I was staggered and could only reply, 'Blimey, that's ten times my weight! You could have got rid of me ten times over.'

And isn't it a fact that here we have the underlying problem with dieting and fitness. It's not just a one-off thing. You can't just tone up the muscles and reduce the waistline and then forget about it. In truth, you've got to pursue the whole business with a will and dedication and that's what worries me. Does this pursuit eventually knock all the fun out of being alive anyway? I mean, have you studied the expressions of inveterate joggers and marathon runners – oh yes, they're mighty healthy, but do they look happy? Surely, there's got to be fun in all things – for that is why we're here isn't it? – to enjoy the world and all that's in it. So let's enjoy the funny side of fighting the flab.

The basic diet, irrespective of calories, kilojoules, high and low fibre, poly or unpoly whatever they call them and all, consists of a very, very simple piece of reasoning:

Eat what you don't like,
Drink what you don't want,
Do what you'd rather not,
And all will be well.

Unfortunately every line is true, but I'd love to be the guy who invented unfattening chocolate and ice cream – I could name my own price for it.

Along with the reasoning, of course, must come a little exercise and the best exercise of all for slimmers is slowly turning the head from side to side when offered a second helping.

Oh yes, we'd all like that iron will, wouldn't we? But in our own humble little ways we try to be strong. Like the lady who was offered a rather large fruit and iced cake and was asked:

'Shall I cut it into two or four madam?'

'I think,' said she, 'you'd better just cut it into two. I don't think I could eat four pieces of that.'

Then there was the lady who tried several different plans: The Z diet – she would never eat anything beginning with Z, and the A diet – only foods beginning with A – A pork chop, A plateful of sausages, A large portion of chips and so on.

But above all, there was the very sensible lass who let reasoning, not panic, determine her outlook on life.

'I know I'm over eleven stone,' she smiled, 'but in reality that doesn't mean I'm fat – I'm just too short for my weight.' Now there's a positive approach at last. There's an example of sense prevailing over false illusion. There's the basis of our fight back against the people who for years have determined how we should look. At last there's hope for all. At last we have a battle cry: 'Out with "keep fit and healthy" – in with "keep fat and happy".'

This will really chuff my pal Joe (second name withheld to protect myself from a pounding). Joe in his time has been many sizes and many weights. Anything up to thirty stone – occasionally reducing to sixteen stone.

'I do my best, but the weight gets back on when I'm not looking,' he explains. 'It's a killer with clothes. I mean my underpants don't have elastic, they have a Swish rail. It got so bad that I had to get my ears pierced so the rest of the family could watch the TV. My wife does her best for me. She even takes my false teeth with her when she goes shopping, so I can't eat between meals.'

'That's a fact,' chips in Dolly, 'he's a caution if you don't watch him. I've told him, if he doesn't behave, I'll sentence him to the ultimate punishment – three months in a cake shop with a muzzle on.'

Good-natured banter and every line designed to ease the stress of worrying over body shape. Joe even has a wardrobe of suits that range in size from his smallest to his largest shape and all are neatly pressed and ready for the increase or decrease that moods can bring. He's tried counselling and has begun to believe that 'it's all in the mind'. He obviously lies abed many an hour working out the roots of his problem. The more he hears or reads, the more intense is his logic. One day Joe came up with a stunning bit of logic that is only born of desperation:

'I reckon my trouble is I'm suffering from bulimia but I keep forgetting to throw up.'

Joe's a load of fun then that's what they say about fat (sorry! circumferentially challenged) people. They have to be jolly because they can't fight and they can't run. But I think my pal was born to be funny. Who else would come out with this wonderful line, 'They asked me to diet down to my original weight – but that was only seven pounds.'

Anyway, for the moment let's leave Joe in his own personal duel with himself and his figure. After all, when he reduces to sixteen stone, he's delighted. How many more of us can say that?

No, let's move on to the serious business of losing (or

in some cases gaining) weight and the various aids we can bring in to help ourselves. We can, for instance, look at positive slogans:

1 To lose weight, eat only what you can afford.
2 If it tastes good, don't eat it.

At all costs, we must ignore the cheap and incorrect tips we receive from 'somebody in the office'. Do not, repeat not, fall into the trap of believing:

1 'If you don't enjoy the food, it's not fattening.' It's amazing how people can eat cream cakes while saying they hate them.
2 'You can't put on weight if you eat whilst jogging.' Don't try it. It's not true and it's awfully messy.
3 'No matter what you eat or drink, as long as you eat a grapefruit after it, you will not gain an ounce.' Hey, if you believe that one, I've got a bridge to sell you.

Forget the erroneous advice, particularly from people who look overweight themselves. Instead, face the facts. Putting on weight owes a lot to the calorie content of our intake and the quantity of our intake. We're going to look at both in turn but, of the two, calories are the major problem. You see, calories have a terrible habit of hiding on you. Do you know what I mean? You eat a massive meal, swill gallons of wine and liqueurs and for two days, you're the same weight as before. Then, just when you're not looking, bang! You've put on five pounds. Why? Calories – calories are sneaky. They lob weight on by the bucketful, but when it comes to taking it off, they renege on you. Trouble is, we're not built the proper way. If only we'd all been made like an ex-manager of mine, we'd have no trouble controlling our intake.

Billy, my manager for some years, could, and often did eat for England. His penchant for food, Guinness and gin and tonic was legendary. Billy could feel 'a little peckish' straight after a full English breakfast. Billy once drank seventeen large gin and tonics, interspersed with bottles of Guinness, and remained standing because the whole lot was for free. But Billy had an ace in the hole. Billy knew when he'd had enough of anything. Billy had a magic jacket. To look at, it was a simple double-breasted blazer, much like any that you see in a crowded high street during business hours. On him, on a good day, the jacket buttoned neatly and gave a straightish cut to his jib. But, let the man overeat or drink and the jacket would rebel, and refuse to fasten. Now I'm not talking about being tight. The damn thing just wouldn't meet in the middle – not just as a double-breaster, but as a single-breaster. Talk about a coat of many colours. This coat could read minds, or at least stomachs – or so it would seem. In reality, it was all down to the man; he would physically swell up on the spot like a bullfrog and leave the table several inches wider round the belly. Probably, his world-record ballooning happened in a Chinese restaurant in Chesterfield (oh yes, Billy got around), when he ordered and totally cleared 'Letter B', which was a meal for four with rice and chips. I don't know whether you've tried it, but it's almost impossible to *carry* a portion of 'Letter B', never mind eat it. Still, it kept him quite full till teatime. My undying memory of the man, though, is that after every banquet, for surely you couldn't call them meals, he'd order a cup of tea and flick a sweetener into it. He was convinced that somehow the sweetener helped cancel out the calories.

You see, we're back to those calorie things again. You'd need to be a Philadelphia lawyer to work out the rules governing calorie intake and output. Suffice to say that you never seem to lose them as easily as you gain them. Of course, you can control them, although that in itself is a work of art. At a very poignant moment in my life, I realized that my shape and habits would have to change – here I was – forty-three years old, miles overweight, drinking pints of beer with great aplomb and smoking like a chimney. (Funny how we have to use comparisons to describe our habits. 'He ate like a horse, drank like a fish and then was sick as a dog – he's not human.') Anyway, I was set to play Buttons in pantomime. 'Easy,' thought I, 'done it half a dozen times before, just dig out the old scripts and costumes.'

But what a shock. The scripts were still funny, but the costumes had shrunk. Unbelievable that crimplene or the like can shrink in a wardrobe. The shoes were a bit tight too. Surely leather doesn't shrink, does it?

'No, it's you, love,' said Pat, 'you look like Tweedle-dum in that outfit. Just look in the mirror.'

It was true. Over the years I'd put on two and a half stone and now looked like your worst nightmare. Beer gut, yellow-stained fingers from the fags, bulging eyes and eye sockets – yuk! No way to appear in front of Britain's youngsters. Get yourself together O'Connor and do it now. And here I played the ultimate ace, I employed the mind against the body. You've heard of the 'feel good' factor? Well, I set out to prove that it could override the 'feel hungry' factor. First off was to make a plan. To feel good all the time would require more than dieting. You see, even though you eat nothing (literally), for a couple of days, it doesn't follow that the scales will show a marked loss of weight. No. More than dieting was needed and so I made the ultimate sacrifice – I gave up everything. Smoking, drinking, eating – it's amazing what you can do when you're sick and tired of being sick and tired.

In history there have been martyrs whose names will live for ever, but none ever broadcast their plight – unlike yours truly who couldn't wait to tell everyone, 'No cigarettes for a week – gone off booze. Oh, and by the way, look at the waist band!'

I'd purposely stuck to wearing my larger trousers so that they looked looser and gave an impression of massive change, bearing in mind that when you're miles overweight, you lose more to start with anyway. But how to appease the hunger pangs? Well, I bought a book called, *Count Your Calories* and this became my Bible:

One apple	– 40 calories
One banana	– 80 calories
Celery	– Nil. In fact, you use more calories chewing celery than you gain swallowing it. (Even so, I couldn't bear to live a celery-controlled life, could you?)
One slice of bread	– 70 calories

So my life took a mathematical turn. Counting calories, counting smoke and drink-free days – recording poundage. I became an expert at weighing food, checking calorie details on tins, finding low calorie but filling meals and shunning my old-time favourite obsessions. I kept out of pubs, so the temptation of a pint wouldn't lead to the craving for a cigarette. I had all my clothes laundered to lose that tobacco smell. I even – honestly – bought trousers an inch, or even two, too tight so I would 'grow into them'. Do you remember as a kid having a period of years when your clothes never actually fitted you properly? You were either growing into them or growing out of them. All this came flooding back to me. Even shoes were becoming slacker. I was getting less breathless going up stairs. Gone were the jocund remarks about old habits.

In the old days on stage, I would borrow a lighted cigarette from a member of the audience, take a drag and say: 'Thanks, I'm cutting down on cigarettes. I only smoke after meals now. I'm down to forty meals a day.' And people would smile – sometimes. But the line had to go.

Now it was the jugular which was my guest. The ultimate holy of holies would be where I'd settle and not an ounce less. I would be the slimmest I'd ever been (not counting my original weight of six pounds) and people would stand and stare. All the aids to helping to lose weight would be employed. Water tablets, you know the kind that expectant mothers or people with high blood pressure often take. I tried some of them. Not recommended. All right for a day or two – you lose a pound or two, but you never stop running to the loo or feeling thirsty – vicious circle – no good.

I tried drawing on memory and recalled that in the callow days of my youth there was a garment advertised which guaranteed to 'slim down the fat parts'. Stephanie Bowman I think was the originator and it was more or less elasticated underwear. Whether it worked or not I know not, never having tried it, but I did try my own version using plastic bags and bin liners. To be fair, it felt as if it were doing some good, and I did sweat a bit but there's something not right when you're in a supermarket and everybody else is standing listening to you rustle up and down the aisles

– and the *smell*!

Still, desperation brings out the best and worst in us all. After plastic bags I settled for a heavy tracksuit and a few miles of jogging. This worked well and felt as if I were doing something positive, although I always ran with the hood up so I wouldn't be recognized – just in case my reserves of energy ran out and I folded in a heap. You see, it's always been my nightmare scenario that a jogger, purple-faced and boggle-eyed suddenly grasps his chest and murmurs, 'I hope that's cramp' and I don't want that to be me.

However, once the jogging habit set in, it gave rise to a constant need to be on the move – no more short car rides, walk to the shops. No trouble in having to go up stairs and down, and back up again because I'd forgotten something. No more lounging in chairs – now sitting bolt upright was the norm. The world was all right again. The tastebuds were returning after years of being battered into submission by Will's Woodbines and Benson & Hedges. Even the sense of smell was being aroused and I could make out beautiful aromas from cooking pots in all directions – actually this was a bit of a drawback to the main plan.

All, or nearly all, was well. The main problem now was hunger and fear of fainting. Again, the old memory box came to my aid. Fill up the stomach with as much as possible, and provided it's not loaded with calories, it will pacify the pangs. You lovely readers will not be old enough to remember an unusual product which I think came from Sweden. It was brilliant in its conception and made the stomach feel full whilst also containing special vitamins. It probably exists today but, being independent, I decided to use my own version of the elixir. To my aid came the old standby – porridge. It's amazing how much of the stuff you can eat without putting on weight and boy is it good for you, and yes it certainly fills you up. Thank you, Scotland, for pure unadulterated nourishment and assistance in our battle against cholesterol. Mind you, a country that has given us haggis and mighty heavy-duty whisky owes us something more.

Along with the goodness of porridge and the calorie-controlled intake of beans on toast and poached egg on toast, I discovered the perfect antidote to the craving for cigarettes. In the past, I'm sure we have all tried killing the pangs with chocolates, sweets, bon bons, anything. My own personal favourite used to be mint imperials and aniseed balls. Suddenly, though, I came across diet wine gums. They're in every chemist's and they don't contain more than a calorie and a half each – suck 'em all day. So here was I, Mr Exercise, Mr Porridge and healthy foods and Mr Diet Sweets. Add to this decaffeinated coffee and tea and you having the makings of the biggest bore in town. Even I began to notice it. Every conversation I got into was eventually switched to my well-being and martyr's sacrifice.

'Do you remember when Arsenal beat Liverpool at Wembley and Charlie George scored that brilliant goal?'

'Yes I do, mind you in those days I'm surprised I remembered anything. My brain was numb with booze and fags and my weight – well, let me tell you how I put that right ...' and on and on and even on ...

Looking back, I must have been hell for Pat to live with. Mr Vain, looking for praise at all times and for ever droning on. The only good thing is that it does force you to persevere through all the cravings because you daren't let anyone know you couldn't keep up the effort. On the way, of course, nature, as only nature can, does inflict the odd injurious slight – like my hair falling out! OK, not in handfuls, but very obviously in bits here and there, and thinning too. Hairdresser to the rescue please. A pal of mine, Ray, a fine exponent of the art of scissory (or whatever it's called) recommended a course of vitamins.

'You're draining vitamins from your system with all this dieting and the body is reacting to it. One of the first things that is affected is the hair,' he said.

Immediately my thoughts went to my mate Joe. Did his hair constantly come and go as he went from 30 to 16 stone and back again? I must resolve to contact Joe, just in case, and put him onto the course of tablets I used. Vitamins A, B, C, E, G – goodness knows, I took them all. And they worked, but with a side effect. As the hair grew back, it changed from silvery grey to its original black – giving me the look from behind of a superfit-skunk. Nearly killed the stage image. But other than that, all was well. The weight went down to a very fine 11 stone 4 lbs and then – horror – it kept going down and I couldn't stop it: 11 stones, 10 stone 12 lbs, 10 stone 10 lbs – what to do? Had I gone too far never to return? Maybe this is what haunts Joe when he's at his 'pale shadow' 16 stone. What I learned was not to panic. The same route that took you down must bring you back. Don't rush into an orgy of self-indulgence but increase portion size and wait for developments. It worked, thank God, and I levelled off at 11 stone 5 lbs. And there I've stayed, more or less, since. But then I got to thinking, Wasn't I lucky that I didn't go too far – to the extremes that others still go. When only matchstick-thin bodies satisfy their wants? And are they happy or are they still craving more and more weight loss? Is anybody really satisfied in this world? Doesn't much always want more – or in this case less? You know, it can be quite a serious business getting fit, so let's jerk ourselves back to the corblimey for a while with some not so true, but should have been, stories.

Like the two little girls in the bathroom. 'What's that?' inquired one, pointing at a set of bathroom scales.

'I don't know,' said the other, 'but don't stand on it or you have to give up sweets.'

Or the tale of the two men shipwrecked on the desert island with the gorgeous blonde model. After many weeks, they decided that the chances of rescue were nil and that they'd better make a go of living together till old age.

'Well really,' said one, 'we should think seriously about which of us should pair off with the lovely Michelle.'

'Indeed,' agreed the other, 'and, with her approval, I've devised a plan which should satisfy all and help us to lead a fit and healthy life in the process.'

'Whatever is best for the common good is all right with me,' smiled the lady.

'Well,' said the brainbox, 'we'll toss up for who shares Michelle's company. Winner takes the lady, loser becomes the cook. And, to be scrupulously fair, there will be an option for change. If ever the winner complains about the cooking, he will lose the fair lady and become the cook himself.'

'Agreed,' said the other, already planning to cover the worst eventuality.

Coin duly tossed, the worst happened for the latter.

'OK, I lose – fair play,' he grimaced. 'So cook I shall be. You two just get on and enjoy yourselves.'

Off gambolled Michelle and 'brains', whilst Mr Unlucky went straight into Plan X. Slowly and precisely he picked his way around the beach and forest, collecting all the most horrible ingredients he could find. Mouldy seaweed, rotting carcasses of birds, broken shells, feathers and bird droppings. Armed with this deadly fare, he boiled a huge pot of water and threw the lot in – talk about the witches of *Macbeth*. Hour after hour, the sickly brew bubbled and gurgled, gradually beginning to look like the potion from *Dr Jekyll and Mr Hyde*. By teatime, all was ready. Over the sand skipped the two carefree ones to be greeted by two heaped platefuls of grub. Mr Brainbox, hungry as a hunter, grabbed a spoon and dug straight in, chewed for a second or two and then spat out the whole lot.

'Aarrgh,' he spluttered. 'This is disgusting, it's filth, it's offal, it's garbage!'

'Yes?' beamed the other expectantly.

'But,' muttered Brains, 'cooked beautifully!'

I'd guess the story offers a way, if only a drastic one, of ensuring the loss of weight.

Generally speaking though, nature has its own aids to regulating our appearance. Provided we put in enough daily effort in terms of walking or even running, and provided we don't go totally overboard in the eating and drinking stakes (you know – no sparks from our knife and fork), then we should remain in relatively good shape. Good habits generally breed good feelings and good health. And this applies both to the losing and the gaining of weight, because it not always to lose weight that people strive. There are those who must try to keep up their intake to prevent them becoming too thin. Overwork, stress, pressures of business, money problems – all the symptoms of today's way of life – all can cause unwitting mortals to neglect their well-being. Meals are missed, or hurried, or unfinished. Too much fast food, not enough vitamins, not enough variation, too much caffeine, too much alcohol – indigestion, ulcers, weight loss – bad feelings, bad health. We must be aware of our physical needs at all times – even in the most dire of circumstances.

Take the suspected smuggler, hastily arrested at a foreign airport, handcuffed and pushed and pulled about. Arraigned before a local judge and sentenced to be detained in the local cesspit jail until trial. Terrified and woebegone, he was thrown into a dank, cold, unlit cell. Bare stone walls, no windows, no sanitation. Only a piece of lice-ridden sacking to lie on. Sobbing at his fate, he fell into a deep comatose sleep – the sleep of the wrongly accused. A grating and banging sound suddenly roused him and he saw a small metal panel in the bottom of the cell door being drawn back. Through the hole was thrown a lump of stale green, rock-hard bread, followed by a rusty mug full of dark brown, sludgy, warm water.

'Why, oh why?' he wailed to the empty cell. 'Why me Lord? I mean why me, of all people?'

As if his cries were a trigger, the most amazing thing happened. A brick suddenly disappeared from one of the walls about six feet up, and a voice called, 'What's the matter pal?'

'What's the matter? What's the matter?' moaned Mr Innocent, 'I've been locked in here on a trumped-up charge. No right of appeal. No one to help me. I haven't eaten for two days and all they've given me is a cup of horrible brown water and a slice of green bread.'

'That's terrible,' said the voice from next door. 'But they always do that for the first week. Then it gets better. I mean, you want to see what they give us old lags. I've got my plate here and it's full. Bacon, sausage, beans, fried bread, three fried eggs …'

'My God,' said the newcomer, 'I'd love a fried egg.'

'All right,' said the neighbour, 'pass your bread through and I'll put an egg on it for you.'

Slowly the bread went through the hole, and without another sound, the brick went back.

Oh dear. The pain. The sorrow. The anger. The frustration. But isn't it just human nature? Much wants more. Even at the basest of levels, the eyes can become too big for the belly. Still, an enlightening experience.

But before we round off this piece about thinking thin and the consequences of it, let's remember certain basic things. Too thin can be just as bad as too fat, and who's to say what suits us best? Beauty is, thank goodness, in the eye of the beholder and if we remember that, then all becomes easy. Don't hang around with people who think your weight is wrong. Mingle more with those who prefer your present shape to one that's too much trouble to maintain. Avoid critics, because what do they know? Snide comments and back-handed compliments have no place in your life. You don't need them, you don't have to stand for them. You know the type?

'Some people are built like Greek gods – you're built more like a Greek restaurant!'

That's not for you or me. Better that we dwell on the positive side of things. Remember that the greatest sex goddess of all time, Marilyn Monroe, was not a sylph-like lady. Never was she a size ten, or a twelve. But as a thing of beauty and allure, the late Norma Jean had no equal. Regard the Venus de Milo – with or without arms – the lady is not petite. She is more comfortably attractive and certainly timeless in her appeal. Better that we should recall these special ladies and remember the more positive side of life, whilst keeping a temperate eye on things. We can't all have everything we want all the time, and the person hasn't yet been born who is totally happy with their lot.

I'm delighted to say that over the years I've become a great fan and friend of that very special all-girl act – The Roly Polys. Large in size, appeal and talent, they've got to be one of the most unusual groups in the business –

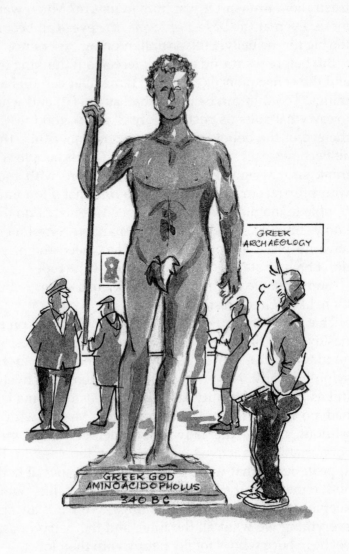

GREEK
ARCHAEOLOGY

GREEK GOD
AMINOACIDOPHOLUS
340 BC

they have to eat a lot to maintain their appeal – what a life! Wouldn't that be a great job – rivalling the all-time envy of all eaters, the Sumo wrestler. Talk about dieting going raving mad.

But enough of this. Time, I think, to mention the part that drink can play in healthy lifestyles. For a start it's just as important in terms of calorie intake as food is. Secondly, of course, in the case of alcoholic drinks the more we take the less control – in all senses of the word – we have. How often does a skinful of beer, enhanced with the odd chaser, lead the stomach to demand a vindaloo, a large portion of fish and chips, or a greasy meat pie and peas? Suddenly, a perfectly normal human being becomes a vacuum cleaner for any morsels that can be spooned, or shovelled, into his chops.

How often, after a long night of groaning innards and burbling stomach acids, have we ended up face down over a sink or toilet bowl and called upon those three great gods of the ill, 'Sid, Bill, Hughie …?'

And then, through a haze of spinning head, unsteady feet and shaking hands, vowed sincerely and earnestly, 'Never again. I promise, Lord, never again!'

I remember the very moment that cured me – well, at least, for a while anyway. I'd gone to the bathroom feeling 'a little poorly – might be a cold coming on.' All the time, I knew it was the heavy stout I'd shipped earlier on, added to the port and brandy that I'd flung down as a 'kill or cure' recipe. There I stood, waiting for the urge to lean forward and retchingly talk to God on the big white telephone, when I suddenly caught sight of my own reflection in a mirror – God, what a vision – enough to frighten the horses! But just then, all changed. Just then, as if by some magician's hand, the mirror moved. Slowly, but ever so steadily, the mirror rose, unaided and began to climb the bathroom wall. What was this? Was it a divine message from heaven? Was it a signal of the Second Coming? No such luck. It was, of course, a case of the mirror staying put and yours truly slowly sinking to the ground. 'Never again for sure this time, Lord' was the last sound I heard before blacking out.

Trouble, trouble, trouble.

3

Eating Out in Style

A very knowledgeable person once remarked that the world had turned on its head – why else would we stay in to see a movie and go out to dinner? Of course the statement is true and owes a lot to modern living. We seem to have gone so far forward that we are catching ourselves up. What was a routine procedure, eating at home, has now begun to be the exception, a time for a bottle of wine and even serviettes. More and more we are conditioning ourselves to visit places of entertainment and food emporiums. How often do we pass on recommendations of good eateries to friends and acquaintances. How discerning we've become in our choice or rejection of restaurants and the like. But why?

Certainly, it is a help to the busy housewife, househusband or working partner to forget the traumas of shopping, feeding, preparing and cooking. Also the modern restaurant can compete fairly well in terms of cost with the household outlay. And when there's the ease of booking the exact time to eat and no worries about washing the dishes – all these are plus points. But surely the real advantage of eating out lies in the excitement of the unknown. Who knows who we'll meet, or what we'll see, in our chosen restaurant? Who knows what will happen by accident or design? Who knows how good, bad or amusing the service will be? Well, whatever, in this chapter, I thought we'd look at some of the things – funny ha ha, funny peculiar and downright odd – that have happened, or are believed to have happened, whilst eating out in style.

Let me tell you straight away that I am the number one fan of all waiters. You see, they never ever get their just desserts (no pun intended). If the food is good we praise the chef and the manager. If bad, we give the *waiter* a dressing down. So it is with fondness and sympathy that I relate a few waiter stories. Like the one about the large person who sat, in fact overlapped, on a chair and began to run through his order:

'Soup, prawn cocktail, melon, fillet of sole, T-bone steak, plenty of chips and two eggs. Cheese and biscuits and to follow two portions of chocolate fudge cake with ice-cream – yes, that ought to do it I think, a good variation. Now, waiter, what do you recommend I should wash it down with?'

'Loch Ness,' came the confident reply.

Oh, I do like those stories, don't you?

'Waiter, I've just noticed that when you brought my meal you had your thumb on my steak.'

'Yes, sir, I didn't want to drop it again.'

A famous Hollywood actress reputedly came second in a bandy of words in the Savoy Grill, London.

'How would you like your coffee, madam?' was the polite question.

'I like my coffee like my men,' she snorted.

'Ah, white and weak it is then, ma'am,' said the waiter.

All good stuff if it's not happening to you. On the other hand, what if you are the butt end of a situation like the man who was served his meal and had just begun to wade in when he heard one waiter say to another: 'My God, he's eating it!'

Generally we deserve the treatment we get – just look at the things we do and say while eating out.

'What do you recommend waiter?'
'Perhaps asparagus tips.'
'Haven't you any Benson & Hedges?'

'I can't eat this steak – bring the manager.'
'It's no good, sir, he tried and he can't eat it either.'

'This oxtail soup I ordered. There's not a lot of it in the bowl. It only just covers the bottom.'
'That's what oxtails do, madam.'

'This 'ere ravioli, what exactly is it?'
'An Italian dish, sir.'
'Well, how would you describe it?'
'It tastes delicious, sir, but it looks like tea bags in tomato sauce.'

'I'm thinking of having caviar 'cos I've heard a lot about it but I don't know what it is.'
'Well, sir, caviar is collection of sturgeons' eggs.'
'In that case, I'll have two, lightly boiled.'

Well, all right maybe some of those lines are a little on the unbelievable side … let's go back to the truth for a moment. I personally witnessed a wonderful incident which I call 'How to lose the girl with one line'.

Pat and I were in a rather nice bistro in Liverpool,

trying our best to stay within a schoolteacher's budget. On a table opposite sat a young Jack the lad, accompanied by a stunning blonde in the most expensive and revealing outfit. Jack was obviously out to impress and launched into the ordering mode.

'The lady would like the lamb cutlets with vegetables of the day and I'll have sirloin steak medium with French fries and chips.'

The 'and chips' did it. Pat and I smiled, the waiter choked on his pencil and the blonde began to plan her escape route.

We told that tale to my pal John and he gave us one back – not a topper but one at least as good. Picture the couple who have taken Auntie out for a meal and can't decide what she'd like. Aunties are like that, aren't they – always making you order things. 'Whatever you say will do for me,' you know the drill.

This hapless pair had rattled through the exotic dishes and were beginning to realize that they were wasting their time.

'I know, Auntie. What about a portion of tongue?'

'Oh dear, no,' she spluttered. 'I couldn't eat tongue. That's come out of some animal's mouth. I tell you what – I'll have a couple of eggs.'

You've got to admit it's quite an original tale and, dare I say, just a little typical of Auntie.

My Auntie Bridie would have fitted the description perfectly – Auntie Bridie who always said that the best salad was an Irish salad: 'Roast potatoes, boiled potatoes, mashed potatoes and chips.'

Maybe a psychologist or some such could explain why we behave so oddly when we're eating out. Bearing in mind we are exercising one of the body's most intimate functions in a very public place. And you would think that we'd be at least half prepared before venturing forth. For surely, there is no greater fool than he who proves it in front of an audience of strangers.

Take the tale of Joe Anonymous who went out to a snazzy eaterie with his pal and spotted the amazing display of crockery and cutlery. 'There's knives and forks everywhere. Big spoons, little spoons, big plates, little plates. Either there's three or four sittings or we're out of our depth here.'

'Don't worry,' urged his pal, 'it's a simple procedure. According to the book I read, you just start using stuff from the outside first.'

An hour later poor Joe was still trying to finish the soup with his serviette.

Nobody can be that dim, but sometimes we all get a little close don't we? And it's funny how a situation can develop and even get out of hand with no help from us. Some years ago when I was a mere lad of nineteen or so there was a joke going round as follows: 'Two blokes went into a restaurant and asked for the menu. On it, in the omelettes section, it had Normal Omelettes £1, Spanish Omelettes £2.'

'OK,' said one bloke, 'you order a normal one and I'll order the Spanish and we'll see what the difference is.'

The two omelettes were subsequently placed before them and, in truth, they looked identical.

'Hey, mate,' said one to the waiter, 'these two look just the same. I paid an extra quid for a Spanish Omelette.'

'Oh yes, I forget,' said the waiter. And snapping his fingers, he shouted, 'Olé!'

Yes, I agree not the funniest of jokes, but here's the tag. A party of my friends and I went to North Wales for a snooker weekend and we stopped at a halfway house for a couple of pints. As we walked in we could hear a record player blaring out a Spanish flamenco tune. One of the lads shouted, 'Olé' and the barman said, 'Heard it!' Jokes sure get around. And so do wondrous tales of waiter *v* customer clashes. In my research for this book (twenty whole minutes, honest!), people were queuing up to pass on 'true' accounts of things that happened to them or more often to a friend or relative. So, not to disappoint them, maybe we should feature a few occasions when the customer wins.

Let's start with the well-worn saga, oft repeated but never unfortunately of any use to me, of the man in the fish restaurant who ordered a lobster. When it was served he noticed one of the claws was missing. On complaining he was told by the waiter:

'You see, sir, it's the way of nature. In the wild, lobsters very often fight amongst themselves.'

'In that case,' said the customer, 'bring me the winner!' Fifteen love to the general public.

Another point, if not two, for the quiet Mr Average who had taken his wife to a posh restaurant for an anniversary bash. Expecting the worst in terms of overcharging he still was not fully prepared to be bombarded with 'hidden extras'. The bill seemed to treble before his eyes and even discounting service charges and VAT, he still couldn't believe it.

'Look here, young man,' he mumbled, 'this bill can't be right. I mean we've only had the basic steak and chips.'

'Ah yes, sir,' said the waiter, 'but there were other things. There was fruit on the table, vegetables, mints, cheese and biscuits ...'

'I know but we never touched them,' gasped Mr Average.

'Agreed, sir, but they were there if you'd wanted to.'

'Very well,' said our hero, finally plucking up courage and seeing the light dawn, 'I'll pay the bill but I'm deducting fifty pounds.'

'Fifty pounds, sir? Whatever for?' asked the waiter.

'Messing about with the wife.'

'But I never touched her,' pleaded the young man.

'No, but she was there if you'd wanted to!' was the self-satisfied reply.

A great answer, a wonderful scenario but not quite what happens in real life. Let's be honest we've all been in similar situations where the cost of eating out suddenly rises to corblimey proportions. Generally we all do the same thing, don't we? We swallow hard and pay – irrespective of the rights or wrongs. I suppose it's sufficient to mark that particular emporium down on our black list and thank Heaven that we could afford to cover the cost. But there are those less fortunate than us who often cannot buy their way out of embarrassment – what happens to them?

Here's a tale of a young lad who was determined not to get wash-day hands.

Picture the scene. A young couple on their first date. She's chosen the venue. He doesn't know till it's too late that it is an expensive, if very nice, restaurant. In a lot of exclusive places, I'm sure you know, the tendency is to give out menus with no tariff on them. The only person who is given a menu with prices is the one the management deem to be the ultimate payer. So it is that the young lad receives a table of fare which includes extras like twenty pounds if you step on a grape or similar item. Rapidly, our hero attempts to sway his love in the direction of the cheaper meals.

'Gosh, the cheese board looks interesting,' is one desperate remark.

'Really, I don't know about you but I'm not that peckish,' is another.

All to no avail. Madam is determined to have chicken

breast and sauté potatoes come hell or high water. And so they are duly served. Coffee flows and an update of the bill is asked for – needless to say the young man's mind is blown.

'Thirty pounds! Thirty pounds! We only had chicken and potatoes,' he protests.

'Ah yes, sir,' smiles the waiter, 'but you had chicken breasts and, as you know, there's only one breast on each chicken. So we had to kill two to make the meal.'

Whilst the hard facts of chicken anatomy are striking the young man's fevered brain, madam suddenly chimes in with an extra demand. 'I think I'd like a cocktail to finish off,' she says sweetly.

'What type of cocktail would that be ma'am? Screwdriver? Tom Collins? Harvey Wallbanger?'

'No, I think,' says she, 'I'll have a Horse's Neck.'

'In that case,' splutters the young man, 'I'll have the back legs. You're not killing two horses.'

Good thinking by the young feller. Saved a possible disaster and possibly saved a little face but you'd not call that a case of the customer winning outright. Here's a tale where he does. Please, please, read this and take it only in fun and never, never try it yourselves. Or if you do, don't tell anyone where you found out about it.

Three well-to-do businessmen entered an Italian restaurant and ordered the very best of meals, accompanied by top-of-the-range wine, with dessert and expensive liqueurs to follow. All was sweetness and light as they puffed on their cigars and cheerily asked for the 'Bill please, *garçon*.'

Only then did the trouble erupt as mutterings burst into argument and argument spilled into shouting and accusations. Gradually the moment became more heated.

'You can't renege an agreement,' roared one of the men.

'I've never reneged in my life,' boomed the second.

'Admit it's your turn and cough up gracefully,' said the third.

'God, it's only money, and it's not as if you can't afford it, Moneybags,' added the first.

'I can afford to knock your block off if you persist,' came the threat.

'Gentlemen, gentlemen,' cried the manager, 'please let there be no ill feeling. What is the matter? Maybe I can help resolve the problem.'

'It's his turn to pay and he's just too darned mean to admit it,' said a red-faced gent.

'Just a minute. Just a minute,' spoke the now remarkably calm 'accused'.

'You two say it's my turn to pay. I insist that I paid last time. Let us not argue the point. We'll settle the matter in true British style by a trial of combat.'

'Trial of combat?' queried one of the 'prosecution'. 'Whatever do you mean?'

'We'll settle it like good sports with a man-to-man competition. A race round the block. Last one home pays the tab. Agreed?' No answer. 'Well, agreed?'

'Very well,' muttered one.

'Agreed,' said the other.

'Right, a race it shall be,' beamed the first. 'Mr Manager, sir, would you be so kind as to start us off. Last one back round the block pays up.'

Happily the manager stood over the three who were in starting-off mode.

'Ready, steady, go!' he shouted … and never saw any of them again.

So far, we've looked only at some *contretemps* between those eating and those serving. Time, I think, to ponder the other incidents that can happen while out on the town. What of those embarrassing moments that

occur from time to time, when the only possible action
is no action. And when the discretion of the restaurant
staff is strained to breaking point.

Take the tale of the young couple who ordered a
corner table 'out of the way' and spent an hour or so
eating, drinking wine, holding hands, talking small talk
and generally enjoying the pleasures of each other's
company. Suddenly, and for no apparent reason, the
young man slumped in his seat and gradually
disappeared from sight.

'Madam, Madam,' cried the waiter as the young lady
inexplicably took out a compact and began to powder
her face, 'Madam, your husband has just slid under the
table.'

'Correction,' said the girl, 'my husband has just
walked in the door.'

Ah, the embarrassment of being young and just a
little flighty. But what about those supposedly old
enough to know better?

Take the rabbi (here comes a Jewish gag) who, for
religious reasons, had never tasted pork. Over the years
his curiosity began to get the better of him.

What was it like? Why all the fuss about not eating it?
If it was harmful, why didn't it strike down the
Gentiles? Surely, anything that smells that good can't
be *all* bad?

So, one day, he determined to find out for himself. He
chose a restaurant in a town far away from his own and
rang up to order suckling pig with all the trimmings for
the following lunchtime. Next day dawned as next days
do and our hero (or villain, depending on your outlook)
took off in a cloud of dust and exhaust fumes to sample
his treat. He sat at his cosy, out-of-the-way table and
sipped a glass of claret whilst waiting for the feast – no
starter for him, just straight to the main event. Then it

happened, wonder of wonders, out came the waiter with a silver salver. It was placed in front of the rabbi and the lid raised to reveal a beautifully cooked suckling pig surrounded with oodles of vegetables and complete with an apple in its mouth.

As knife and fork were raised to the start position, a voice said:

'Rabbi Greenberg. What are you doing so far from home?' It was a leading member of the rabbi's congregation.

Caught stone dead to rights, our hero offered a feeble, but at least quick-witted reply, 'Ay, ay, the restaurant was highly recommended by a colleague and how right he was – I only ordered an apple and look at all the trouble they've gone to to serve it.'

Probably not a true story – too far fetched. Surely real life is never so off-the-wall. Or is it? My own experiences have never included rabbis or courting couples, but one of my most embarrassing moments happened so totally innocently and suddenly that 'stunned' can be the only description of my reaction.

Pat and I were over in Italy, visiting our eldest daughter, Anne Marie, her husband Rocco and their little girl, Patricia Jade, to whom I've dedicated this book. We'd gone out for a meal and oh I do love Italian food – or even British food cooked by Italians. Pat and I had ordered fish starters, assuming that what would be served would be the main body of fish without the inedible bits like fins and heads, a bit like smoked salmon if you like. But no, oh dear no, on our plates were two complete sorrowful-looking creatures with all the extremities still attached.

Anne and Rocco meantime were digging in to their pasta starters. While they demolished spaghetti bolognese, Pat and I picked and poked around our fish, lifting a piece of flesh here and there and trying to remove just enough to let us leave the rest without reproach. Soon it was done and, with most of the fish bones on view, we put down our cutlery, whereupon Rocco seized the remains of my fish, broke off the head and proceeded to suck out and swallow its contents. This done, and without a word, he did the same to the other.

Whilst we sat, fishlike with mouths agape, he explained: 'I learned as a boy never to waste anything and the head and brain of the fish are the best part.'

We were too taken aback even to feel ill. All that ran through my mind was – never order fish in this man's company again.

But back to eating in style, which is where we began and time for a positive look at why we choose the better type of restaurant even though the cost is a little higher.

Much as we all love and cherish our fellow man, woman and child, it's not every day that we wish to mingle with them, which is probably why we don't all live in communes. Each person can be interesting and charming in their own special way, but surely there comes a time when we need to have a while to ourselves and our thoughts. So it is with eating. OK, the odd bash in McDonald's or a motorway service station is fine – certainly great fun for the children – but once in a while we all need to be able to relax and watch the world drift by when satiating our appetites.

For a few years, we had a flat in the Earls Court district of London near West Brompton tube station. And my great delight was to walk the mile or two round the block on a summer's evening taking in the ambience and smells of the many outdoor cafés, restaurants and bistros of all nationalities. That one-off special aroma of freshly brewed coffee, the scent of garlic gradually spreading into curry as it floated on the evening air. I'm delighted to relate that in our time there, we ate in virtually all of those places and were never disappointed. But of all the restaurants (I know, it sounds like Humphrey Bogart in *Casablanca*) in that part of London, my favourite has to be Mr Wing's. What service! What atmosphere! What style! The Chinese food is the best I've tasted anywhere in the world. The selection of dishes is second to none. No wonder it is the haunt of many people who wish for only good food, good wine and a memorable evening with friends.

'It's Tommy, look it's Tommy O'Connor' is the usual way I'm greeted when arriving unannounced. 'Tommy come in, how many are with you? Have a brandy with me while you look at the menu.'

I only ever took up the brandy offer once – I lost track of how many I'd drunk, but the bottle was empty when I left. Mr Wing's is a great place to relax, settled back in a cosy corner amongst the foliage of the potted plants and creepers. There's no official cabaret, no extraneous noise, but occasionally there is a moment to make the customer smile. Take the night we popped in after a concert in London. We hadn't booked (*mea culpa*) but the maître d' was doing his best to accommodate us in the most trying of circumstances – a full restaurant. 'Maybe Tommy you wouldn't mind taking the small table on the far side?' he suggested.

'Anywhere's fine,' said I.

'Only, you see,' he explained, 'we have a booking for the large table in the centre. It is that velly famous Mr Crapton, you know' – saying his Ls as only the Chinese can. 'Mr Crapton has been doing a show in town.'

'I know,' I smiled, 'we've just been to see it. He was wonderful. But if I were you,' I suggested, 'I wouldn't use his second name, at least the way you say it. Try

''Ellick'' instead.'

Yes, Mr Wing's has style and my custom for ever, but it's not alone on my shortlist. I mean, if you want the full ambience in terms of 'going out for a nosh' then why not try one of my other favourites – Doyles Restaurant. No, not the one where you live, or even the one just a few miles away. I'm talking about Doyles in Sydney, Australia – the one on the harbour that specializes in all things seafood. So what if it takes hours in a plane to get there? Believe me, it's well worth the journey. Nothing can compare with a sunny day in Sydney, walking down to the harbour, past the shops and bars and through the general hubbub, boarding a launch and crossing the short stretch of water past the Opera House and in the shadow of Sydney Harbour Bridge. What a way to go out to lunch! And the food – oh, the food! – squid, prawns, fish of all kinds – and served with chips if you like– paradise under the sun.

'Hang on,' I hear you cry, 'Aussie's a bit far to go just at the moment – I live in Macclesfield and only have weekends off' – in that case, wait a while, take early retirement and treat yourself to a holiday – go on, spend the grandchildren's inheritance while you're still alive.

Meantime, my best advice is to search your local area for the better places to eat. When we lived in Liverpool I was recommended a restaurant called Churchills in the city centre. As the referee was my local bank manager I gave it a try and it was superb – a great choice of dishes, a relaxing atmosphere – hey, and plenty of parking space. From that day forth, I've always sought advice when eating. When we came south to live, my main link with London eateries was Dickie Hurran. Dickie was a great character. Top producer/director for the Bernard Delfont organization, the best lighting man in the business.

There's an old pro entertainer's story of the comedian who said to his pal, 'I went out for a meal with Dickie Hurran last night.'

'Oh really,' said the other, 'what did you have?'

'Corned beef sandwiches.'

'Corned beef sandwiches – is that all?' gasped the friend.

'Ah yes, but beautifully lit,' was the reply.

Not true, not true, never would be. Lovely Dickie has passed on now but his lighting plots will go on for ever. So will his advice. Both on and off stage the man was a mine of invaluable information.

'You want a good meal, son? I'll take you for one, bring the good lady too.'

So Pat and I were treated to the 'full Monty' at Simpson's-in-the-Strand. Now there's a place to visit for style. I've never tasted Scotch beef as good in my life – wunderbar (as they might say in Macclesfield) – it almost made me forget the starter. On second thoughts, that would have been too tall an order. Because the starter was one of my all-time favourites – tripe and onions – for years I'd watched my grandparents and parents eat raw tripe and thought, 'They'll go straight to heaven, because they're already doing their purgatory on earth.'

But then I tasted cooked tripe and onions and realized what a wonderful treat I'd been missing. I could eat it till the cows come home – or even later. Particularly the way it's presented at Simpson's – always with style. There's even a certain style about their refusal to serve it.

Only once did I fall into the trap. 'Scotch beef medium. And to start with tripe and onions,' I smiled, folding the menu over without glancing at it.

'Not today, sir. No tripe and onions today,' said the waiter.

'Sold out?' I asked innocently.

'No, sir. It's Monday, don't you know.'

Of course, of course, Monday – never gave it a thought. No tripe on Monday, wouldn't be fresh left over from the weekend – what a fool I am for forgetting the day of the week.

You see at Simpson's they serve good food as a matter of principle and you could say it's my principal reason for eating there. When I do, I toast the memory of Dickie Hurran who used to refer to me as 'the mover'.

The reason, very quickly, is that in the very first ever show he produced with me in it, he was giving instructions to the choreographer.

'So the dancers split eight each side, O'Connor comes down the steps, they meet in a line and he goes into the routine with them.'

'Just a minute, Mr Hurran,' came the voice of Tommy, my road manager. 'The boss doesn't dance. He's a talker, not a mover.' Laughingly, Dickie saw the point and left me to my own devices as a 'talker', but as 'the mover' he never forgot me.

I'll never forget him either, or his advice. One day in his honour, I'll order corned beef sandwiches in Simpson's – but the lighting is going to have to be right.

4

Me and My Diet

I was at a fondue party a while back and was bemoaning the fact that I'd reached the ripe old age of fifty-five.

'Away with you,' said the hostess, 'why you're still only middle-aged.'

And I got to thinking, 'How many a hundred and ten year old men do I know?'

Bless her heart, I knew what she meant, I was not yet old, but I was no longer young – but didn't I know it, and prove it every time I opened my mouth.

'You see, when I was a lad ...' There I went again. Looking back through time-tinted eyes, 'we never had the problems we have today ...' etcetera, etcetera ... and so on ... zzzzzz boring.

Nature dictates that people of forty-something and older will always decry things that are modern, and loudly praise the things of their youth – whether they were good or bad. It usually starts with prices.

'Eighty pence for a bag of chips? *Eighty* pence. My God, that's sixteen shillings in old money! When I was a kid you couldn't *carry* sixteen shillings' worth of chips, never mind *eat* them.'

'Five pounds for a seat in the cinema. When I was a lad you never paid more than five pence. And you could get twenty cigarettes for sixpence and beer was threepence a pint.'

All true, but what we old 'uns don't add is that we didn't have two halfpennies to bless ourselves with.

If money is the opening gambit in our look back in time, then food and drink are never far behind. See how I've already mentioned chips and beer – the most staple of staple diets of my youth. These, along with winkles, jellied eels, bread and dripping and jam and bread were the absolute necessities of my early days in Liverpool. These and various types of stew, of which more later, were pure ambrosia to youngsters growing up in the austerity of post-war Britain.

We hardly saw sweets of any kind, and those we saw were severely rationed. So no bull's-eyes, chocolate bars, toffees or fudge. Instead we made do with a delicious mixture of cocoa powder and sugar which we carried round in paper bags and constantly dipped wet fingers into. Actually I was lucky in this department because, being an only child, I didn't have an older sister interested in American soldiers. You see, older sisters would purloin the cocoa ration and use it to stain their legs when they couldn't get stockings.

If cocoa was a sweet luxury, then bread and jam was a sweet necessity. 'Jam butties' as we called them on Merseyside are part of the folklore of the forties and fifties. If there was plenty of jam the bread was cut thin. If the jam pot was low, you ended up with a 'doorstep' – a huge wodge of bread with a fine veneer of the good stuff on it. Jam came in various flavours as it does today. Damson, plum, blackcurrant and, my favourite, strawberry. Today, however, the manufacturers freely admit that there are additives to the main ingredient, but that a great percentage of the jar is real jam. In our day, God only knew what went on our bread. But there were legendary stories of people working in the 'jam factory' whose job it was to work a lathe turning out home-made stones to put in the jars to prove the stuff was real.

Those were the days.

Yes indeed, days when we'd never seen a banana except being eaten by the chimp in a Tarzan film. Days when curry was only the smell that enveloped the Chinese seamen coming off ships at Liverpool dock. Days when Camp coffee was all the rage. Can you remember that special taste? It hooked me on coffee for life. Days when ... and so on ... and so on.

Without doubt, times were harder then, and any little extra was regarded with esteem far outweighing its value. But I don't think that was a bad thing. Sure, we ate too much fat. Sure, we used too much salt and OK maybe we put a little too much sugar in our cups. (I remember a priest visiting our house once who put eight teaspoons of sugar in a cup of tea. He was never invited again.) But then we were living in times when it was hard to know where the next meal was coming from and so we had little self control.

Different days followed when prosperity came and goods became more plentiful. Rationing ceased, and shops filled with wondrous things. Green jelly – I'd never dreamed you'd ever get green jelly. Real eggs and not tins of powdered stuff. Different and exotic-looking fish – not just the smelly salt fish of days gone by.

Yes, the world was all right again and I enjoyed

growing up. Even school dinners began to improve – now that was a real eye opener. In the early days there was a basic format for meals which worked on the principle that nothing went to waste. On Monday there would be great globs of meat-like substance set in very thick axle-grease gravy – casserole surprise. If that didn't take everyone's fancy it would be represented on Tuesday. This time the globs were minced and covered in burnt mashed potato and called shepherd's pie. What was left over re-appeared on Wednesday. This time it was coated in custard and re-named prune delight. But those days were going. Now sausages made their appearance. And not sausages made of breadcrumbs and fillings. Suddenly there was real meat in the bangers.

On the dessert front we'd never had such times – spotted dick, jam roly poly – all served with thick, if sometimes burnt, custard. Do you know I can still recall that one-off smell of burnt custard – funny how it hangs on isn't it?

So imagine, if school grub was so much improved, how wonderful home cooked meals suddenly became. Soups suddenly became a source of wonder. We'd always had chick pea and watery tomato, but now came chicken noodle – ah yes, oodles of noodles, and extremely nourishing. Oh boy for noodles and hello to alphabets. Alphabet soup – now you could spell it. What a game it was sorting out the various letters. I don't know about the rest of Britain but I could never find letters B or Q – maybe they were too difficult to link up. Also there was a dearth of Ms. I think they were so flimsy they broke up into As and Ns.

With the soup in packets we were also regaled with other dehydrated meals. Add water and you could have paella or chicken supreme. Amazing how stuff would

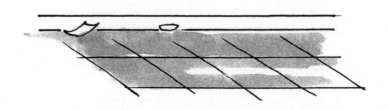

expand before our eyes. It took me back to the words of my grandmother, 'In my day, you could make a meal out of nothing if you had the stuff.'

My adolescent years witnessed the arrival of Instant Whip dessert – just add water or milk. Instant Cake Mix – just add water and an egg. Instant mashed potatoes – just add – well, you know the rest. No more would dinner need to be predictable. In fact, with portion packing, each member of the family could eat something different. Except of course on Sundays. Sundays were special and eating revolved around the family joint. And what a variety of joints we had to choose from all of a sudden: beef, lamb, pork, ham, chicken, turkey. Blimey, the options were endless as were the trimmings: apple sauce, mint sauce, Yorkshire pudding, parsnips, turnips, carrots, peas, cabbage, cauliflower – boy, oh boy. And potatoes – you name the style and Mum could cook it – boiled, roast, fried, mashed, sautéed, whichever you chose – you'd always remember 'the way that Mother used to make it'.

Mums made pies too, remember? apple, gooseberry, rhubarb, cherry – all tasty, all nourishing and all made of real fruit – no manufactured stones in these pies, nor in the jam. What a life, and how quickly it dampened the memories of the bad times. Times that would be almost totally forgotten except for the odd memory jogger. Like my cousin John. He was born, like me, with a sweet tooth, the kind of tooth that nothing quite satisfies. In my heyday I've demolished a half-pound of chocolate fudge and still not been sated. John was just like me, but curious with it. And curiosity and food are an awesome combination.

So it was that Aunt Rose left six-year-old John at home while she popped to the shops. Unfortunately, on her way, she met a pal who kept her talking longer than normal. Meantime, the little feller went rooting around in the kitchen. Here he turned up a bottle of dark red liquid which he took to be strong lemonade. To complement this he was lucky enough to turn out a drawer and find a small packet of chocolate. In slightly longer than a trice the lad had quaffed the lot and began slowly to stagger around the house in a desperate search for the loo. Or in his case, three loos, for that's how many he could see in his condition. By the time Aunt Rose returned she found she was dealing with an incontinent drunk. The red fluid had been rum, and yes, you've guessed it, the chocolate was Ex-Lax. Remember the old gag? 'They told me to go home and relax. I thought they meant those little chocolate things. I haven't relaxed since!'

But the good times came and they still prevail. Who was it who said we've never had it so good? Harold Macmillan was talking of general material wealth but he could easily have concentrated on food and drink. You name it, the shops had it. If they didn't have it they could order it. If the prices were so dear that demand fell, then prices were re-adjusted. If small shops could not handle the low profit margins, the supermarkets sprang up, followed by hypermarkets, followed by huge discount warehouses. Hurray for the good life and welcome to the land of plenty!

Of course the trouble with good times is they can become too good. Whoever coined the phrase 'you can't have too much of a good thing' didn't really understand human nature. Better to have said 'a little of what you fancy does you good', or 'moderation in all things'. For left to ourselves we mortals can become overwhelmed by the good life. Easy come means lack of effort. Lack of effort eventually leads to laziness – and sloth is one of the deadliest of the seven deadly sins.

Although a life of leisure is probably what we all desire, we must pay a price and keep paying no matter what. Just as a car needs constant maintenance, and don't forget a well run engine is much more efficient than one hardly run in, so our bodies must be treated with respect and given careful overhauls and regular work outs.

Going from adolescent to married man, albeit a fairly active schoolteacher, I gradually began to forget the basic elements of life. Good diet, regular exercise, good sleep patterns and, most of all, moderation in all things. These are the fundamentals of good and healthy living, but how easy it is to gradually let them slip through our fingers. My problem began with trying to fit in too much in one day. Working in the morning, a few pints of beer at lunchtime, working in the afternoon and then trying to 'relax' by going out for two or three hours in the evening. 'It's good to unwind' someone will always say. The trouble is you can unwind so much that you can't stand up…

When you're young the body can absorb an awful lot of punishment without too much of a whimper but gradually the rot sets in. Constant work, continual 'unwinding' and general lack of fresh air and exercise wear down the system and a feeling of tiredness and lethargy set in. Just try drinking four or five pints at Sunday lunchtime, then eating a huge Sunday lunch and then staying awake for the rest of the day – impossible. The result is usually a deep coma-like sleep around three o'clock which disrupts the pattern of the rest of the day – not recommended. Some of the best advice I ever had came from sportsmen, whose trade depends solely on the health of their bodies. 'When you're tired son, you'll do one of two things – eat or sleep. If you can't sleep for any reason, then be careful what you eat.' So spoke a very successful boxer who knew what he was talking about. Since then I've tried to avoid situations where tiredness forces the pace of my life. Better ration the day to equal amounts of eating, sleeping and exercise.

So with all this knowledge of what is right and wrong and all the choices of what to eat or not, how am I coping today?

Well, considering I was born and brought up in a different era, I'm not doing badly. Remember that when I was a lad (oh! oh! here he goes again) things weren't so bad for you as they are now. Sure, we ate a lot of fatty things, bread and dripping for a start, but the quantities were of no great consequence because they were barely above starvation level. Sure, we smoked and drank, but for some reason they didn't seem to take the toll that they take today – or maybe we just didn't want to hear about it – probably the latter. Certainly we exercised more, simply because no one could afford a car and few could afford a bicycle.

Today, because of increasing pressures of work and life in general, there is a tendency to take the easy way out when it comes to eating and exercise. How often do we make do with sandwiches, packets of crisps, chocolate bars and anything else that can be gorged down while we are on the move. Often we give no thought to calorie intake, cholesterol or fat content, because we don't appear to have time to bother. The answer is that we should make the time, or at least attempt to organize our day to fit in the good habits that our bodies need. OK. On the day it can be a problem when the heat is on and the flak is flying, but time can be found the night before to plan the forthcoming twenty-four hours – even if we do it while falling asleep. Over the last year I've forced a plan upon

myself, much sometimes to my own annoyance. Healthy foods like porridge, wheatgerm, fish and fresh vegetables, salad and decaffeinated coffee have gradually replaced my old-time favourite grub. You see my greatest loves used to be fried eggs, bacon, sausage, black pudding, white pudding, fried bread – in fact the entire contents of a greasy spoon café, together with any type of stodgy pudding, chocolate fudge cake and bucketloads of cream biscuits and sweets. Now that they've been left out of my life the difference is startling. The blood pressure is back to normal, sleeping patterns are more regular, a new energy drives my body and suddenly I have time for all things. It's as if someone has connected me to a metronome and then eased back on the tempo.

Combined with better eating, of course, must come better drinking. I mentioned decaffeinated coffee and this replaces a plethora of alcoholic favourites. In my time I've fancied rum, gin, brandy, whisky and always heavy beers or stout. it's amazing how much energy can be fired back into the system when the alcohol is driven out.

Remember the old gag about the man who was breathalyzed? 'Blow into this,' said the policeman. The motorist blew into the bag and when three days later the Russians shot it down over Siberia, the policeman was still hanging on to it, singing 'Nellie Dean'. They took a sample of the motorist's blood and gave it back to him in a glass with an olive in it.

All this is in jest, but just a little too near the truth for comfort. As much as we try to ignore it and no matter how lightly we pretend to take it, life is a once and once only affair. So let's take it steady, and get the most out of the fullest life possible. Let's have fun, let's eat, drink and be merry but do it in moderation. Meanwhile, let's enjoy the happenings and mishaps that can befall the eater, drinker and dieter.

5

Eating Out and
Blow the Consequences

I guess that everybody has memories, both fond and not so, of eating places they have frequented throughout their lives. Generally, and usually because distance lends enchantment to the view, the good outweighs the bad. The 'absolutely superb' are remembered far more than the 'never again'. So it is after deep thought and much note scribbling that I launch into a chapter about the 'one-off, make a note not to do this twice' kind of venues that we've all seen at first hand.

You know the type:

'If you can't smell it we haven't got it.'
'The Cordon Bleu should be cordoned off.'
'The food is so bad that the other side of the menu is a doctor's prescription.'

Funny lines indeed and lines, I'm convinced, that were quoted after unfunny experiences. There's nothing worse than a bad meal, be it served in squalor or luxurious surroundings.

Take the greasy spoon joint. You know straight away that this will not be the Savoy – in fact it's so far across the other side of town that it doesn't even overlook the Savoy. But surely there's no excuse for the food not to be cooked properly. Do you remember the classic meeting of minds across the tea-and-brown-sauce-smeared counter?

'Yes, love, I'd like two fried eggs – one burnt around the edges, the other with a runny yolk. Two rashers of bacon burned to a crisp. Two sausages burned black on one side and raw on the other, and a pot of lukewarm, stewed tea.'

'We can't serve you that,' exclaimed the waitress.

'You did yesterday,' said the traveller.

Sometime in history that story has got to have been true, but why? Surely at any level of catering there's got to come a point when the system reaches a point of stability and all meals come out the same, or maybe that won't happen till robots rule the earth. Or maybe it won't happen until we start demanding good quality instead of enduring bad in the fingers-crossed hope that all will be well. Maybe we should be more like the Americans who insist on the best in terms of service and make a great fuss if they do not get it. There's nothing better than being on a cruise ship or in a holiday resort with hundreds of Yanks. By gum they do have the caterers hopping. But, at the end of the day, doesn't their style eventually lead to chaos? I mean have you tried ordering even a very basic meal in a US eating house?

'I'll have two eggs, miss.'

'And how would you like the eggs cooked? Would you like them boiled, soft and easy for three and a half minutes? Just so, and tender for four minutes? A little harder for five minutes or would you like "eggs all the way" at over six minutes? Maybe you like 'em scrambled with milk, without milk, a little seasoning, maybe even Tabasco sauce? Or would you like them fried, sunny side up, flipped over, easy over, over and out and crispy on the edges?'

'I'd like them scrambled on toast please.'

'Scrambled on toast it is. And how would you like the toast, sir? On white bread, brown bread, granary? Would you like it lightly toasted all over, lightly on one side, blacker on the other ...'

'On second thoughts, miss, I'll just have a cup of coffee.'

'Coffee it is and how would you like the coffee? We have espresso, cappuccino, decaff, Mexican ground ... hey, just a minute buddy, where are you going?'

Perhaps it's as well we don't go all the way with the USA but there must be a happy medium between them and the rest of us. Or maybe someone should compile a list of places to go, or not go depending on taste and value for money. The car industry has a Glass's guide to quality of vehicles, maybe we should compile a similar book, *The Taste Bud and Good Vibes* guide to eating places? You know the idea:

'The chef here can't even spell steak Bordelaise, never mind cook it.'

'In this establishment, the only way to get a good helping of food is to sit at a table near the window.'

'This venue has a very fat dog. Always a sign that the food is bad and is generally sent back and ends up in its bowl.'

Of course our guide would apply to the good as well as the not so good:

> 'In this restaurant, a rare steak is one that costs less than fifteen pounds.'
> 'If you ask for any item less than five pounds, they look in the waste bin.'

The trouble with this sort of guide is that it would certainly print out the highs and lows of a place but, by design, would not have enough space to include the humorous tales which surround it.

In Chapter Four, I mention early days in Liverpool and the effect they had on my diet and regimen. Unlike today, my youth was spent in an era of austerity and 'eat what you can, when you can' in case there was none tomorrow. And during this time, the major influence on me and thousands like me on Merseyside was the sea (whether they were sailors or dockers, my heroes were men of the sea). Men of great humour, long-fused tempers and a wonderfully worldly outlook on life. So, most of all, when I think of funny stories in eating places of less than five stars, I immediately think of dockside canteens and the lads and lasses who work there. Stories like the one about the newly painted sign that proudly boasted, 'Special offer, today only, all you can eat for two pounds.'

'Great,' said Luke, the not-so-brilliant stevedore, 'give me four quids' worth.'

Or what about the café that displayed the sign, 'Thieves about. Watch your coat!' in huge letters on the main wall.

'Hey pal,' grumbled one sad sack, 'I've spent so long watching my coat that someone's pinched my steak.'

Or then again there was the tale of the young tea boy

sent from a distant work point with a vacuum flask to get the tea for a gang who were trying to finish the job early, without a tea break, so they could get off to the football match. 'The boss wants four teas in this flask please, love,' he said to Fag Ash Lil the waitress, 'three with sugar and one without.'

But I think my own personal gem from those halcyon days involved a spit and sawdust caff which I used for many a happy lunchtime while working at the Herculaneum dock. I seemed to spend for ever one summer helping to unload bales of cotton from a ship called *The Settler*. She never seemed to get any higher in the water although we took out thousands of bales daily. We had an old codger working with us whose nickname was the Home Secretary because if you didn't keep an eye on him, he'd sneak off home and leave you to all the work. But he was a mine of information regarding all things maritime. He even knew, be it by the tides or not, what was happening in the world of catering. 'There's a sugar boat just come in yesterday, so you'll be able to stand your teaspoon up in the cups today,' and he'd be right. It seems that whenever there was a glut of anything, the dockside cafés did their level best to unload it on you.

But I digress. The reason I mentioned the Home Secretary was because of a particular event which he swore he witnessed – and who am I to argue with a man of the sea?

It seems that one lunchtime a very hungry but very picky docker (is there such a thing?) inquired of Fag Ash Lil: 'What kind of soup have you got today, luv?'

Normally this would receive an answer like, 'Hot' or 'Thick, but not as thick as you' or some such. But not today. Today the answer was: 'Well there's a special one on as a trial. It's turtle.'

'Never tried that,' mused the hungry one, 'I think I'll give it a go.'

'Turtle soup one,' the waitress bellowed through the serving hatch.

But then – 'Just a minute, luv. I've changed me mind. What else have you got?'

'Well there's thick pea,' she replied.

'Yeah, I'll have that,' said Mr Picky.

There then followed the most wonderful of one-line orders ever given through a café hatch: 'Cancel the last order. Hold the turtle, make it pea!'

Whenever I remember the docks, I'm forced to remember that waitress for somewhere she still exists, if not in that particular body form, certainly in the soul of other ladies of the catering profession. And not just here. She lives in the heart of waitresses all over the world. Because theirs is the life of the order, the cancelled order, the change of mind, the unwarranted complaint, the back-handed compliment. But theirs is also the world of the brilliantly witty put-down, riposte and 'wish I'd said that' retort.

For years I used to use the gag about the Irish bloke who went on holiday to New Zealand on his own (for some reason, that one line used to raise a chuckle – never ever found out why). Anyway, back to the plot. Bold Patrick one day entered a small, not-too-greasy-spoon joint and asked for the full Irish breakfast.

'I'll have two eggs, bacon, sausage and fried bread please, me darling.'

'I'm sorry,' explained Miss New Zealand, 'you can have eggs and sausages and there's plenty of bread but I'm afraid we've no bacon today.'

'What? What?' muttered a bewildered son of Erin. 'No bacon? All the sheep in New Zealand and you've no bacon?'

'Government cutbacks,' smiled the girl. And we'll never know whether she thought he was joking or he realized that she was joking.

None the less, of such stories are legends made and every era throws up its own particular bunch of them.

'Waitress this steak's funny.'
'Well laugh at it.'

There's a terrible smell in this restaurant. It must be the drains.'
'Can't be, sir. We haven't got any.'

We really do ask for it, don't we? It's as if the need to satisfy an appetite goes hand in hand with the need to stumble into a world of comedy and absurdity. I remember when there was a major scare over the safety of eating beef. My good lady Pat decided she would take no chances. Until things returned to normal she would shun the flesh of cattle and seek other alternatives. This eventually reached ridiculous proportions when she decided to treat the grandchildren to a fast-food evening out.

'Now, what'll we have, kids?' she inquired. 'Beefburger and chips with plenty of ketchup,' came the excited reply.

'No. No. Not beefburger, not just at the moment anyway. Let's see if we can find something else just as good.'

Scanning the menu, Pat suddenly was hit with the brainwave of all time.

'There it is. That's what we'll have. No beef – instead we'll have hamburger' – and they did.

It took a while to explain through tears of laughter that hamburger lent its name not to the pig, but to the nationality of the beef-loving inventor. Poor old Pat –

not a good day, but a moment of innocence which could happen to anybody – well almost anybody.

It certainly happened to the comedy legend, Tommy Cooper, but then most things did tend to happen to that wonderfully talented man. Tommy was a big fellow, six foot five, an ex-guardsman. Big he was, and awkward in appearance, but when he moved he glided like a skater. Slow he looked and at times befuddled and bewildered. But underneath that comic mantle there lived the quickest of wits and the most razor sharp of brains. Big eating was not Tommy's forte, he was more of a picker. But this never got through to those who served him grub and many a one found to their cost that they should have done some research before challenging him on it.

I was once in his company when he ordered, 'Just a small steak and a few chips, luv' of a flustery, fluttery type lass of sixty-plus years. When the steak finally arrived, it was massive. It was in the size category of 'a horse couldn't jump over it' and surrounded by what looked like a year's supply of French fries.

Tommy, deep in conversation and firing out the funnies, hardly registered the outrageous proportions of the meal, but picked and poked at it for a while before pushing the plate away. A plate which still contained ninety-eight per cent of the original quantity. Then about two minutes later, it started:

'Well, look at that. That's disgraceful that is. That's disgraceful,' wailed Miss Sixty-plus.

'What is? What is?' inquired the bemused Cooper.

'What you've left on your plate. That's disgraceful letting all that go to waste. That's a sin that is.'

'What are you going on about?' pressed the funny man.

'I'm saying it's a sin for you to leave all that lovely food. What about all the starving people in the world?'

To which Tommy gave that 'stop them in their tracks' reply:

'Name me one of them!'

Nice one Tom.

But the fun goes on and it seems there's always a new source. Be it what is said, or what is written, food always brings out the oddest of odd situations. Sometimes it gets me to thinking and when it does, I have the oddest thoughts.

How come, no matter how you slice a pizza, it's always too hot when you start it and too cold when you finish it? Odd that, isn't it?

How come that sign writers never think before writing signs? You know what I mean. At one time I had a lot of work in clubs in the Preston area and each night I would pass a garage whose sign writer never quite got his message over. The first night it said:

Cheap Tyres

Next night:

~~Cheap~~ Tyres Cheap

Followed by:

~~Cheap~~ Tyres ~~Cheap~~ Cut

Then a totally new board:

Tyres Slashed

In the end, I stopped reading them.

That's the thing with signs though, they seem to scream out for some knee-jerk reaction. What about the beauty in the roadside caff:

'Any meal you like, you name it, we serve it.'

'Give me a crocodile sandwich and make it snappy.'

It probably resulted in a version of the old standard: 'I see you can serve any meal I name,' said the businessman.

'Yes, sirree,' chuckled Mr Owner, 'name away.'

'All right then,' smiled the customer, picking up the gauntlet. 'I'll have elephant's trunk on a toasted bread roll please.'

No reaction from Mr Caff; just a turn on the heel and an exit through the serving door. This was followed by a wait of two or three minutes before the owner returned with the bad news.

'Sorry, guv, but we can't do your order.'

'Thought so,' beamed the businessman. 'No elephant's trunk.'

'On the contrary,' apologized the guvnor, 'out back we're up to our knees in trunks. But we've run out of bread rolls.'

What amazes me is people's reactions, so quick and so sharp to what appears to be quite normal notices or statements. Maybe it's because they bring out the negative side of me and so I can't see the fun for the pessimism. Too late I see the humour when it comes from someone else and then I think, 'I wish I'd said that' or better, 'Just wait till next time and I'll say that.'

Take the very basic quote in the café menu:

One egg   £1
Two eggs   £1.50

Now I immediately wonder, what's wrong with the second egg – stale? Tiny? What?

Whereas my pal Ray read the same item and said to the waiter, 'Here's 50p, I'll have the other egg.' See what I mean?

So now I make a point of saying very little in eating houses and just pricking up my ears and enjoying the flow of one-line gags and true utterances.

'Waiter, I don't like all these flies in here.'

'Tell us which ones you don't like and we'll shoo them away for you.'

'Waitress, there's a fly in my cake.'
  'Give it back. I'll give you a currant.'

On and on they roll, seemingly bringing mirth from the most obscure sources. Even the more serious subject of bullying can be dealt with humorously and once and for all. Take the classic situation of the small chap in the corner of the transport café, quietly preparing to tuck into the full shebang of eggs, bacon, sausage, fried bread, beans and all the trimmings. Through the door came three Hell's Angels bikers, complete with leathers, studs, garishly decorated helmets and obviously out for trouble. Spotting Mr Quiet in the corner they made a bee-line for him. Before he could mutter a word of complaint, they'd smeared his entire meal with brown sauce and emptied the salt cellar on top. Almost at once, they'd emptied the entire sugar bowl in his tea mug, and stubbed out their collective cigarettes in his toast.

'What do you think of that, Skinny?' they laughingly inquired.

Saying not a word, the little fellow rose and walked slowly out of the establishment, accompanied by gales of laughter from the trio. Fun over, they approached the counter to order.

'See him?' one of them said to the proprietor. 'What a wimp. Not much of a man was he?'

'No, and not much of a driver by the looks of it,' smiled the guvnor. 'He's just run a juggernaut and trailer over three gleaming motorbikes.'

Eee, I do like that story. But to round off, let us move away from the obvious venues and consider for a wee while the other places where we, even unwittingly, partake of sustenance – pubs.

Let's refresh our memories as to what else these places have to offer. Close your eyes and picture your local on a busy Friday evening and it's almost for sure that you'll see a bar full of bowls. This one full of crisps, that one olives, another with nuts – why, it's a veritable tuckshop before your eyes and all free. OK, so they're also there to make you feel thirsty, but at least they're free. Behind the bar, hanging on cards of many different hues, there are peanuts, cashews, roasted, half-roasted, pork scratchings, you name it, they've got it. Usually at the end of the bar, or somewhere strategically placed within eyeshot or smell, there is a heated compartment full of rolls, pies, pasties and puddings. In most pubs now there is also a pub grub menu featuring all manner of meals and desserts – ready in a trice and all good value. Yes it's a fine world, the world of pub eating. And to it all must be added the genial banter of mine host.

'It says here in the menu there's a special offer today. A pint, a pie and a kind word – two pounds. Is that right?' inquired the stranger.

'Yes, indeed, sir,' replied the manager.

'I'll have some of that I think,' said the customer warming to the offer.

On being served, he remarked, 'Well, I've got the pint and the pie. But what's the kind word?'

'Don't eat the pie,' smiled the boss.

That reminds me of a pub in Lancashire where I once worked as a singer. In the days before satellite TV, computer games and the like, when hostelries used to provide their own entertainment, it was a regular thing to be booked for a 'free and easy' night where anything went. Pie and peas would be the usual dish of the day. Nothing quite like it to help keep down a gut full of beer. Variations to the norm could include: spare ribs and butter beans, a great Liverpool favourite, or Lancashire hot pot and red cabbage.

Various sports and activities would be put in train for the three or so hours of good drinking time. Darts, skittles, even dominoes were played at no less than Olympic level, while the odd round of sporting quiz questions would tease the memories of the buffs along the bar.

Now we've all seen TV extracts of the ridiculous lengths to which some Japanese contestants will go in order to win competitions, staked out in the blazing sun, having their Y-fronts filled with spiders – all weird and wonderful stuff. But none of it compares to stuffing the human frame with food, just to prove its capacity. Do you remember the film *Cool Hand Luke*, where convict Paul Newman takes on a bet as to how many hard-boiled eggs he can eat? The scene is stunning in its reality and leads me to believe he really did polish off the bucketful. Well, in Lancashire, they don't go in for swallowing that many eggs – they'd rather concentrate on pies – and I do mean pies. Big 'uns. Not your thin and weak stuff – pies you can get your teeth in and, if you're not careful, *leave* your teeth in. Pies full of good honest grub. Not like the old gag:

'Waiter, there's a worm in my pie.'

'That's not a worm, sir, that's fat.'

'No wonder it's fat, mate. It's eaten all the meat.'

No, we're talking heavy duty pies that only the North can produce. Pies that put skin on your back like velvet and muscles in your eyelids.

So, picture the scene. Two strapping lads facing each other over a mound of good wholesome food – a mound almost as big as the butter mountain.

Tension fills the air and the crowd wait with bated breath for the word 'Go' from Elsie the barmaid, a girl who hardly ever says 'Stop' (sorry, couldn't resist it).

In they tuck with feverish abandon, crusts and meat crumbling in their molars and crumbs flying everywhere. Ten pies apiece, twenty, twenty-five and then, as if hit by lightning, the jaw of Fat Sam clamps shut and stays shut. Slowly he slumps in his chair, pie unfinished, eyes glazed, all fighting spirit drained.

'And the winner,' bellows the landlord, 'after a technical knockout, is Jason, our new and undisputed champion.'

Cheers and applause fill the air as Fat Sam's cornermen begin the inquest.

'Twenty-five and a half pies! I mean that's nowt in terms of bulk. I can't understand what happened,' said one.

'Neither can I,' agreed the other, 'I mean, in rehearsals this afternoon, he ate forty-seven.'

All right, all right, not true – but wouldn't you like it to be?

6

Don't Say 'Take It Away'
– Say 'Take-away'

If there is what can be described as a halfway house
between eating out and eating at home, it must be the
Great British take-away. I don't know, but I'm prepared
to gamble that learned men would trace its origins back
to the days of the hunter seeking prey. The challenge of
leaving the house in search of new and exciting meals –
or even just the plain old tried and trusteds is
irresistible. From caveman to City gent, from dinosaur
to the beasts of the jungle, the common bond is need of
food and need of variety. How boring a life it would be
if the same dish was placed in front of us every day,
every week, every year with no alternatives.

No, oh dear no. Not for us humans the world of the
mundane. Better the thrill of the hunt and the
satisfaction of choice. And of course where there's
choice, there's scope for accident or bumbledom,

stupidity or just plain comedy.

Let's begin with a classic take-away tale from the animal world. It involves the king of the jungle, Mr Lion, and his penchant for all creatures great and small – provided they are edible. Have you ever watched a film of a herd of wildebeest being stalked by a lion? The herd usually numbers hundreds and any half-dozen could trample the predator to death. But they don't. They know he is only searching for one victim and that will be the weakest who can neither struggle nor run away. So we see a multitude of wildebeest backing away saying to each other, 'It's all right, he only wants Charlie.'

Well, take that story on a stage and we have Leo busily chomping away at what's left of Charlie when on the scene comes a gorilla. Making a noise in the undergrowth to distract the lion, Mr Gorilla races out, grabs Charlie's remains and beats a swift retreat. Hot on his heels he can hear the lion, roaring and booming and crashing through the foliage.

Suddenly the gorilla bursts into a clearing to find the tent of a white hunter. Dashing inside he puts on the hunter's hat and spectacles, places a pipe in his mouth, grabs a copy of *The Times* and sits cross-legged pretending to read it. In an instant the tent flaps open and there stands a red-faced, out of breath lion.

'Have you seen a gorilla?' he asks.

'Do you mean the one that ran away with the lion's lunch?' replies the gorilla.

'Blimey,' says the lion, 'it's not in the papers already, is it?'

Fortunately, our quest for sustenance is never quite that dangerous. But, nevertheless, every sortie can be a challenge, can't it? You see, there are so many options today and as you know, we mere mortals are always open to a little variety when it rears its head. Why else would we, over the years, take great delight in swallowing portion after portion of things like whelks, winkles, mussels, cockles and jellied eels? Good grief, if we had to describe them to a Martian as sources of protein, we'd probably make him physically ill. All manner of things tickle our fancy at meal times, or even in between. Hot chestnuts were always a big favourite in our family. The smell, the feeling of warmth when clutching a paper bag full, always added to the enjoyment of a winter's evening. It's a little like that with hot dogs isn't it? How often has the aroma from a hot dog stand, that special smell that you can never get anywhere else, suddenly made it essential that you buy one? Not in a minute. Not later. Now, now, *now*. Your whole being cries out for that roll and sausage and onions, and mustard and ... well you know what I mean, don't you?

And if mere hot sausages can create such a craving, what chance have we got against the 'eat me now' attraction of the greatest of all take-aways, fish and chips. Let's face it, we're talking here about a dish that has swept the world with its popularity. There's nothing else quite like it for smell, taste and, be honest, value. I wonder if you can remember the first time you tasted it, or even the first time you shopped for it. My earliest recollection was a small chip shop in Bootle. The manager, Joe, had flaming red hair and was as thin as a chip himself. His wife, Rose, was a big lady. In today's language, she was probably a little in excess of eighteen stone. Unlike today's scientific explanation of obesity and its relation to hormones and other amazing things, Rose's problem was she couldn't stop eating the product.

Whether serving, wrapping or frying, she was

constantly picking up chips and scraps of fat and lobbing them into her mouth. You could say that Rose was a great example of what was best and worst in the stuff. But, Joe? He was different. Built like a whippet, Joe was a terrier behind the fryer. Mr Greased Lightning (and I do mean greased). Spuds in the chipper, chips in the fat, fish in the batter, battered fish in the fat. It seemed nobody had to wait more than a few seconds to be served, as if the man had a divine gift of knowing who wanted what at exactly the right time. He could ask you your order as you joined the back of a long queue, remember it, and have it wrapped when you reached the till. Only once did I dare open my paper and check if he was right – he was. Joe was my hero. Joe gave me my first chip wrapped round with a small piece of newspaper, and I ate and thoroughly enjoyed it. Joe made me a believer.

It's just like the first love of your life, isn't it? It's wonderful. It's unforgettable and it's never repeatable. Goodness knows I've tried to recreate the wondrous taste of that first chip, but all in vain. Maybe it was something to do with the taste of the newsprint on the wrapping. Still, it doesn't worry me too much because now, while the quality may not always be spot on, there is so much more to choose from.

Let's start with the basic format. Fish, chips and mushy peas – I mean, what else could you want? Irresistible, totally edible – and calories? Let's forget about calories. (Hey, they cause enough trouble as it is. More about that later.) But in just one simple bag full of fare, there can be so many options. Hake, sole, cod, haddock – the list goes on – fish cakes, scallops, saveloys – how much choice can we handle? And to garnish it all we have pickled onions, piccalilli, gherkins, pickled eggs, pickled … well, there's just no other food like it.

Nothing but the great British take-away can invoke

situations where a housewife complains bitterly about
having to spend all day sweating over a hot stove and
when her husband comes in, she says, 'What would
you like for your dinner before the chippy shuts?'

Ah yes, the great chip shop lines. Where would we be
without them?

'Fish and chips twice.'
'I heard you the first time.'

'The fish won't be long.'
'Well, it had better be fat then.'

'Excuse me, mister, have you got any chips left?'
'Yes son.'
'Serves you right for cooking so many.'

The latter used to be our regular Saturday night piece of
mischief years ago. I suppose the owner was bored stiff
with the same old gag but we liked it.

'Did you hear about the big fight in the chip shop?'
'No.'
'Yes, it was terrible, three fish got battered.'

Oh no, groan, grimace – but we really liked that one –
there's no accounting for taste, is there?

So maybe I can make it all up to you by recounting a
'wish I'd said that' story about fish and chips. As the
tale also involves Americans, and our putting them in
their place, you might just forgive my earlier ramblings.

The story goes that a party of forty-two American
tourists, complete with cameras and videos, were
visiting various parts of the North of England. They'd
seen the Beatles museum in Liverpool. They'd spent
some time in the mining town of Wigan and explored

Wigan Pier. Now they were back on the coach and taking a spin around Blackpool in the day, while waiting for the lights to come on after dark. The browbeaten coach driver was trying to point out landmarks while being constantly interrupted by a loud-mouthed Texan.

'On your right ladies and gentlemen, we have the North Pier Blackpool, one of the longest piers in Europe,' he explained.

'You call that a pier?' sneered the Texan, 'that's a pier? Why back in Texas, we have piers ten times that size.'

'On your left,' went on the driver wearily, 'on your left, ladies and gentlemen, we have Harry Ramsden's Fish and Chip Shop, one of the largest fish and chip shops in Europe.'

'Mercy me. Is that what that little biddy thing is? A fish and chip shop?' said the big mouth. 'Believe me, boy, in Texas, we have fish and chip shops twenty times that size.'

Just then the coach passed Blackpool Tower.

'My God,' gasped the Texan, 'what's *that*?'

'That, sir,' smiled the driver, 'is a vinegar bottle from one of your fish and chip shops.'

I'm delighted to find that fish and chip emporiums are still booming and indeed blossoming out. Now, of course, it's possible to make specific orders of fish by pound sterling – from tiddlers up to Moby Dick. Many, many shops with names like The Happy Haddock, The Friendly Plaice and Chummy Cod are springing up and it seems that, as in my youth, they are generally run by that same combination of one large person and one lean. Whether they used my Joe and Rose as a blueprint or whether they too were just a throwback to two similar people in Victorian times, it's hard to know.

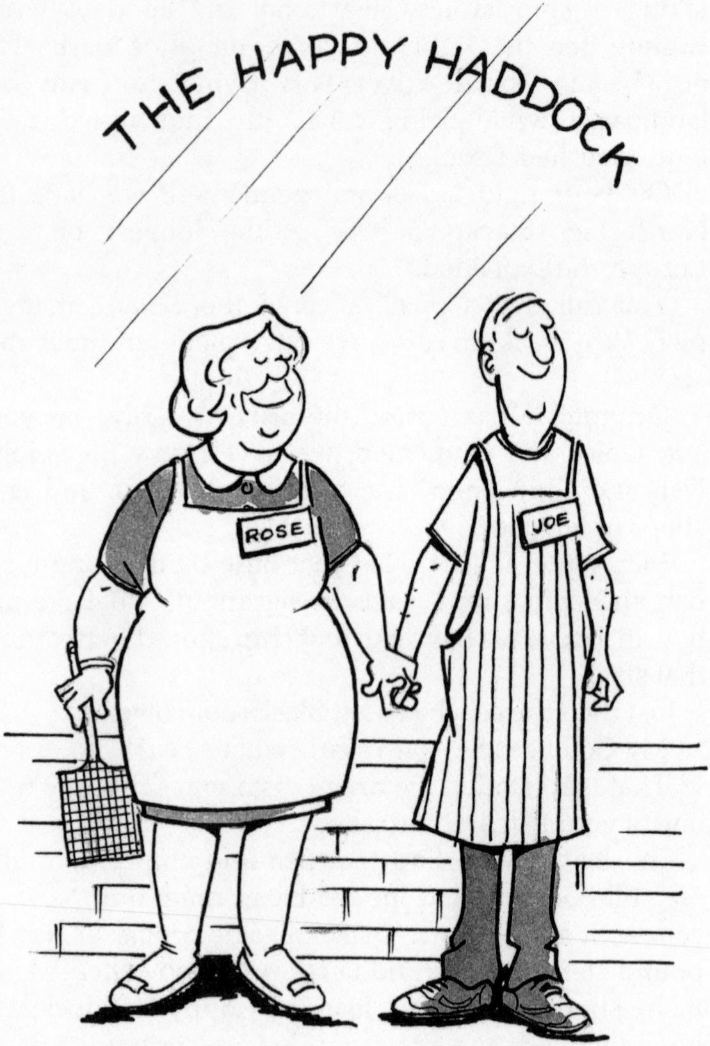
THE HAPPY HADDOCK
ROSE
JOE

What is for certain is that, even in today's world of built-in obsolescence, rush and push and executive stress, one of the grandest feelings in the world is walking along a seaside promenade on a warm summer's evening with a paper of fish and chips in your hand. It can lead to so many funny happenings, because the brain is relaxed and the mouth runs out of control. Do you remember the story of the two old ladies, gorging chips and sauntering along, who suddenly spotted tram lines in the road (hey, and they're still there)?

They inquired of a passing policeman, 'Excuse me, officer, if we put a foot on those lines, would we be electrocuted?'

'No missus,' he replied, 'only if you threw your other leg over that wire up in the air.'

Ah, the seaside. The seaside, of course, here am I talking of all things seaside and not mentioning one of the greatest of all take-aways: candy-floss. I mean, where would the children be without that pink fluffy mess which looks so inviting, wispy and angel-like? There should be a parent's charter which warns the unwary of the dangers of allowing children a stick full. We've all seen the consequences haven't we? To start with, it's almost impossible to bite off just a small amount. The whole blessed thing tries to unravel and come off at the same time. What misses the mouth, and with children that's usually a great deal, ends up all over faces, hands, T-shirts, hair and immediately melts into pink superglue which no power on earth can wipe off. Still, what reaches the taste buds is fun, and the whole process is part of growing up.

A long way into this chapter on take-away grub and no mention yet of foreign food and the way it has swept the nation as if from nowhere. Nationalities from far distant lands are now quite happy to share their culinary arts with us. You name the country, you name the dish, and all is yours, complete, if you like, with chips. My first introduction, in the sixties, was to Chinese fare. I remember my first portion of take-away curried chicken with chips – a strange, yet tantalising taste which hooked me on curry for ever.

I wasn't fussy on the way the chicken was served. Just a portion of breast, complete with bone, laid on top of the chips and smeared with curry sauce. I found that required a little too much effort to eat from a bag – too messy as well. Eventually I settled and still do for curried prawns – easier to manage and tastier – particularly with fried rice.

Whatever the meal though, the Chinese food wave took off in a gigantic way. Suddenly, there were take-aways everywhere. It led my pal, Ray, to remark, 'If the Chinese put something in the curry on a Saturday night, they could take over this country on a Sunday.'

And of course that was before the Indian take-aways sprang up. Then the Thai, Cantonese, Japanese, kebab houses and so on. All good stuff. All healthy nosh and all a source of humour. Remember when the Vietnam war ended (OK, so you're not as old as me) and people were fleeing that country? This conversation supposedly took place in a Liverpool bar: Arthur to pal, Jim, 'I see in the paper that there's a boat load of Vietnamese refugees coming to Liverpool.'

'Yes,' said Jim, 'God knows what their chips are going to taste like.' Sums it up, doesn't it?

The stories are legion because where there's life, there's hope and where there's life-giving fodder, there's always going to be humour. Even produce from the USA is not exempt from a little gentle mickey-taking. Particularly when it comes to my pet love – signs. When Kentucky Fried Chicken first made it big in Britain, it was like every new product: the world and his wife wanted to try it, and this led to a small fall in business for the other take-aways. Only to be expected I know, but hard to live with if you're in the trade. However, it's no problem if you're in the trade and sharp-witted. I loved the sign, handmade, that appeared in a Lime Street chip shop just days after the KFC storm hit town: 'Morgan's Kentucky Fried Chicken. If Colonel Sanders had had our recipe, he'd have been a general.'

Just the start of a long list of rib ticklers that persists today. They've even reached the hallowed halls of the pub quiz league:

Q.   Which number is the odd one out?
     9, 12, 15, 17, 18, 21.
A.   No, it's not 17 – it's 12. 12 is the only one served with rice.

You want to see the reaction to that in a full pub …

Yes, the world of the take-away is now a full part of British folklore. We make references to it out of hand, and without a thought:

'He's so stupid, he thinks a Big Mac is what Columbo wears.'

'My wife's not too good. She had a Chinese last night and she says something must have disagreed with her. I said it had more nerve than me.'

It's hard to think back to those days, not a million years ago, when there was still wonder to be found in the ordering of food at will and even by telephone. All you of the modern generation take it so for granted that the voice on the other end of the line will cook and wrap the exact choice of food that you have made. And that it can be collected in your own time, or even delivered to your door. How life has progressed.

Back in the mid-seventies, we moved from Bootle to a new house in Formby some miles away. Pat was very proud of our dormer-bungalow and wasted no time in inviting as many of our friends as possible to come and give it the once over. On our shortlist was a very talented Radio DJ, Billy Butler – still, I'm happy to say, number one on Merseyside. Billy and his family duly arrived at O'Connor Towers and the grown ups sat and jawed while the youngsters frolicked on the lawn.

Teatime came and Pat produced a menu from our local Chinese take-away – would everyone like to order? This was done, bearing in mind that the bill of fare included British as well as Chinese meals. Choices all completed, I ran the order through and was asked, 'How long you want?'

'Fifteen minutes please,' I replied.

At the appropriate time, Billy and I whizzed round in the car to collect it, and pick up a bottle of wine. Eagerly, the kids tucked into their various selections and happy was the banter. It wasn't till the following morning that Billy's wife rang up laughing to inform us that the children couldn't wait to get up and spread the word about dad's *nouveau riche* friends.

'They're that well off that they have their own chef. Tom just rings him up and tells him what they want and what time they want it. Gosh, I wish my dad was that rich!'

More than twenty years later that story fades into the category of old news when you take into account the ease of ordering meals today. Name the item and someone somewhere will get it to your door. Pizzas delivered by folk on motorbikes or even push bikes, arriving at such bewildering speed that you feel they must have a 'keep hot' strapped to their panniers. There's no end to the choice and in big cities like London the mind boggles at the weight of hot food that is being freighted around at any one time. Generally speaking of course, the deliveries correspond to the telephone orders – but not every time. Take the great pizza mystery of Royal Ascot Golf Club.

Before we begin, let me tell you that it's taken many, many months for me to get up the nerve to repeat this story. Even now I shiver with fear lest the unhappy victim reads this book. But, when writing a book on the fun of food, I feel it my duty to include all humorous tales, particularly the true ones. So here goes.

Some time ago, my son Stephen, my best pal, John O'Neil and myself played a three ball at Royal Ascot. Turning towards the clubhouse at the end of the round, we decided to put our clubs in the cars before we went in. In the car park, next to Stephen's van, was a Honda with the boot lid slightly ajar.

'I think we ought to slam it shut, don't you?' I opined.

'Just as well,' agreed John. 'But maybe we should check the guy hasn't left his keys in the boot first.' Sensible.

'I'll do it,' said Stephen. 'It'll give me a chance to get rid of this.'

Out of the back of his van he brought a five-week-old pizza still in its delivery box. Ordered and then forgotten about, it had lain festering in the dark of his spare-wheel casing, only now to see again the light of day. But not for long! With a deft flick of the wrist, the stale order was lobbed into the Honda and the boot slammed down on it – gone …

Into the clubhouse we strode, hardly daring to think what would happen when the Honda driver eventually got home and discovered the added baggage. Two coffees and a genial swap of gags later, we were preparing to leave when a bloke in a group in the corner got up and went out, bidding all a fond farewell. Gone was he, but only to make the world's fastest return. Glassy eyed and out of breath, he rushed in blurting:

'You won't believe this. You won't believe this!'

'Go on – you've just found out you've won the lottery,' a pal guessed.

'No, no, stranger than that. A bloody sight stranger than that. Someone's been into my car.'

'Oh no, what have they taken? Your clubs, the radio?'

'No, that's just it. They haven't taken anything. But they've left a pizza,' he babbled.

'They've what?' inquired a barfly.

'Left a bloody pizza,' assured Mr Honda.

'What, they broke in and left a pizza?' asked one.

'No. That's just it, they didn't break in. It was in the boot, but no sign of a break-in.'

'Well, that's weird,' said another, 'maybe they had a car similar and their key opened your boot. Maybe they made a mistake.'

'No, I've looked. Mine's the only Honda in the car park. I can't believe it.'

By this time, we three were in convulsions of laughter, but hardly in a brave enough mood to own up to the prank. So we let it lie. I was tempted to go out with the mobile phone and ring the club to check if the pizza we delivered was to the customer's liking. The others talked me out of it.

Instead, we left, still choking back the laughter and little realizing the lengths to which the story would stretch. Obviously, the recipient would re-tell the tale and possibly embellish it a little, but who was to know how much. By the time the golf club bulletin was issued at the end of the month, the pizza was reported to have been piping hot. Now we certainly can't own up for fear of making Mr Honda into a liar!

Strange things happen every day and I always wonder what embellishments will be added when the episode is retold. It would be interesting to be a fly on the wall when mere human reasoning tries to explain another human's behaviour. I was once on a train and, unwittingly, became an eavesdropper to an odd conversation – well at least the tail end of it as a couple were rising to leave.

'So, what did you do eventually?' asked one lady.

'What could I do? I thought to myself, If he's not got the marmalade, there's no point, so I just left it hanging there and ...' And then they were gone. But what was hanging? Will anyone ever know?

Something similar, but not perhaps so weird happened at my behest a long time ago in Yorkshire. Let me explain. Whenever you and I talk of take-aways we quite naturally picture food, hot or cold. It's not so often we think of drink. And yet, how else would an off-licence thrive if it were not from take-out orders? Of course, there are occasions when an off-licence can't be found, or funds will not stretch to paying that little over the odds amount. So what to do then? In my courting days, I thought we'd found the answer. As a struggling young student teacher, I used to save the cash I made from part-time jobs, including maths tuition, in order to have a once-a-month bash in Pat's home town of Keighley. There, I made many friends like Brian and Sheila Middleton, Tony and Cath Bland and loads more. Collectively, we didn't amount to a wealthy crowd but by gum we had lots of fun. It was that wonderful age when people could have a real skinful of beer and never become aggressive – only dafter.

Although we could shift quite a bit of ale, our demands hardly ran to buying a barrel. So we sought a substitute, and Brian found it in a gallon jar of cider. We gaily supped the contents and then went round to the local to refill it with best bitter. The manager took it in good heart until he realized how awkward it was and how long it took to funnel in the brew.

'Just this once, and never again,' he muttered less than benignly.

Needless to say, the gallon went in double quick time. But now what to do? I forget who suggested it but the resulting vote was a positive yes to sending Michael, a teetotaller, to another pub with the gallon jar. And, as a back-up, we gave him a tin bath which probably held five gallons. None of us dared go with him in his pick-up truck, but we were left to think of the pub manager's reaction to the new 'customer'.

Apparently, the conversation went something like this:

'Can you fill these up please, landlord? I'm not sure how much the bath will take.'

'By God, you've got some thirst on you,' said the host.

'Oh no, I don't drink. I'm teetotal. But you never know who you'll meet,' replied Michael. 'By the way, could you give me a hand to load it on to the truck?'

What must the awestruck guvnor and guests have thought as Michael sped off into the moonlight?

'Doesn't drink, but carries six gallons around just in case he meets someone,' you can imagine them saying.

'Mind you, I've heard of something similar in Leeds.'

'And Manchester.'

'What is going on?'

Nothing quite like a good mystery I always say. Although sometimes it can be very disappointing when the whole essence of the mystery is explained. Be honest, wouldn't you rather a magician keep his secrets to himself and not spoil the illusion? Still, there's always someone who will persevere to the bitter end. I recall a fine Liverpool-based comedian called Billy Moocho, who does a great Jewish act. In a world of a million different gags and one-liners, I always remember Billy's tale of the little Yiddisher boy who went to the local ice-cream shop and asked for a large cone.

'You're Jewish, aren't you?' asked the proprietor.

'Yes, sir,' replied the youngster.

'Then I'm sorry, son, I'm not serving you.'

Upset and near to tears, the little feller went running home to explain what happened.

'I can't believe this,' exclaimed his dad. 'How can it be in this day and age that we still have discrimination? Wait till I get my hands on this guy!'

Round to the high street flew dad and son and entered the shop – Cohen's Ices.

'Who's the boss here?' asked the father.

'I am,' replied an extremely Jewish-looking man.

'Cohen's Ices and a face like yours. You're Jewish, aren't you?' reasoned the angry one.

'That I am,' said Mr Cohen.

'Then how come, my boy is Jewish and you won't serve him ice-cream?'

'My friend,' beamed the owner, 'have you tasted our ice-cream?' Enough said.

There we've done it again. Sneaked quietly into a story about another form of take-away. We forget about the ice-cream trade, don't we? And yet we order millions of them every day. And what a choice there is. I'd never have imagined in my post-war youth that the basic cornet or wafer of simple vanilla would gradually be superseded by an endless variety of flavours, mixtures of flavours, double-headed cones, cardboard wrapped biscuit ices and the like. Why even the smallest shop has a tray featuring ten to a dozen different colours and tastes, colours and additives. Chocolate chip, chocolate mint chip, fudge, caramel, coffee ... and on and on. That's not counting the smearing of sauces – chocolate, raspberry (we used to call that monkey blood). Then there's the addition of a chocolate flake bar – the 99. And as if bunging things in the top wasn't enough, they've now started bunging things in the bottom of cones as well. I don't know what you have round your way, but there exists a thing called a 'Screwball'. This is a much-filled cone which contains a solid ball of bubble gum wedged in the base to heighten the pleasure as one reaches the end of the treat. I'm told it's now possible to order a 'two-ball Screwball' for double delight. Is there no end to the permutations? Add this to the fact that, in case your day does not include enough time to visit a shop, the man in the van brings the shop to you. Not only does he bring it, but he arrives in a blaze of music so loud that he cannot be denied, and can even interfere with TV reception.

So 'Stop me and buy one' has now become 'Buy one and stop the noise'. Take-away has become 'Take one and I'll go away'. Still it's all in good fun, and harmless to boot. I mean who could claim to have suffered any anguish over such a simple thing as an ice-cream. Well, on second thoughts, there was the story of the lady – you know the one? Well, it seems (according to some obscure bloke who's a friend of a friend) that in Los Angeles not long ago, a lady was passing an ice-cream parlour, when she looked inside and spotted the film actor, Paul Newman, seated at one of the tables. (You could change it to Sean Connery, Tom Cruise, even Lord Lucan, or Shergar.)

Not quite able to believe her own eyes, she thought, 'I'll go in and buy an ice-cream, while I take a second look.'

Up to the counter she strode and ordered a cone while making sure that the great man was indeed the customer. Now what to do? Approach him and ask for his autograph, obviously. Maybe even ask him to pose for a photo. With this in mind, the lady turned from the counter and made for the famous one.

Hang on, she thought, nobody else has gone near him. I'm the only one. I'm going to look a proper idiot. On second thoughts, I won't bother.

So thinking, she left the parlour and stepped into the street. Only then did she realize that she couldn't find her ice-cream. In a fluster she rushed back into the store only to be greeted by a smiling Paul Newman, who said: 'It's in your handbag lady.' It's amazing what we'll do in a panic, isn't it?

And isn't it the basic law of nature that whatever we enjoy most is either bad for us, fattening, or messy? Surely, in our lives, long or short, none of us escaped eating a toffee apple without smearing our faces, hands, eyelids, hair and clothing. How wondrous is the area that can be covered by a dripping ice-cream, or a bar of chocolate? But the great God invention seems ever to spring to our aid with the man-size tissues and wet wipes. Although personally I think we're taking comfort and leisure just a little too much for granted. An example, if one were necessary, is the story of the husband enthusing over the virtues of a brand new microwave oven he'd just purchased.

'You see, love. It can cook what you like, when you like it, in a matter of minutes. It's *so* versatile. It has *dozens* of features to make life easier. In fact, there's things the makers haven't even thought of. Do you

realize that you can now cook a meal, freeze it for as long as you like, years if necessary, then place it in this machine on defrost and it will come out piping hot.' Oh yeah.

But enough of these ramblings. The time has come to round off this particular chapter and, as always, I've chosen a classic story/gag/true happening. Well, if not strictly true, it should have been. To set the scene, I must remind the world that no matter what choices are presented by the multitude of food stores, an expectant mother can usually add at least a dozen more. All fathers will agree with me that there are dishes that only exist in the minds of soon to be mums and nowhere else on this earth.

So, we have the eight and three-quarters months pregnant lady who begged her husband to go to the shops and buy her a bag of snails in their shells.

'Snails? Snails?' grumbled hubby, 'you normally can't stand the sight of them.'

'I know, but I can't explain it. I've got to have them, and I mean right now. And don't call in to the pub while you're out – just come straight back, do you hear?'

'Yes, dear,' muttered dad-to-be and off he set. Duly he reached Mr Fishmonger/Delicatessen and purchased a paper bag full of the creatures. On his way back he decided to pander to the needs of impending fatherhood and dashed into the Red Lion for a swift half.

Deadly. Pal upon pal appeared at his side and each insisted on wetting the unborn baby's head. So long did this go on that daddy in waiting became so pandered that he could hardly speak. Two hours later, he fell out of the pub and stumbled homeward, taking the usual three paces forward, two back and one to the side. After what seemed eternity, but was probably even longer, he reached the house. As he lurched to the front door, he let go the paper bag and it fell to the ground, bursting open and scattering snails in all directions.

Just then, his beloved opened an upstairs window and bellowed, 'Where have you been till now?'

Quick-thinking hubby looked down at the snails, waved his arms in their direction and said, 'Come on lads – nearly home!'

7

Home Cooking

Eating habits, like charity, begin at home. From the instant we are weaned on to solids, we humans begin to form loves and hates in the food and drink department. Our tastebuds seem to have a greater recall than our brains in as much as they can instantly reject flavours that we can't remember having sampled.

Or maybe it's just that the natural progression of things passes down a dislike for cabbage, spinach and castor oil, and an equal craving for bacon sandwiches, pie and mash and chocolate fudge cake. Wherever and however our eating habits are formed, it is certain that they will go with us to the grave unless we force a major re-think.

Personally, I've always maintained that mind can win over matter any time. Never have we been given a craving that can't be controlled by force of will – cigarettes, booze, caviar, custard, are all addictive to those who choose to be addicted. Equally, people can refrain from certain dishes while forcing themselves to partake of others. My motto has always been 'we eat because we have to, not because we want to'. Now, while this might sound good, unfortunately, where it falls down is in the fact that I can't, and *never will* eat kippers and custard together. I know it probably seems picky to you, but I draw the line at warmed up kippers and custard.

Now, before you ask how I came across such a weird combination of foodstuffs let me explain that the early part of my life was spent in the company of a very strong-willed Irish grandmother – Biddy McGrath. Biddy had lost one husband in the First World War and married a second just before the Second World War. She'd raised six children – 'None was smaller than fifteen pounds at birth' – and knew all the ways of force-feeding kids.

Her basic rule was that, if presented with a dish often enough, the spirit of the child would weaken to the point when swallowing their pride meant swallowing a much burnt offering. So kippers and custard, smelling and looking hideous, eventually had to be eaten, but with a firm vow never to reject any further meals for fear that they be combined to make a formula totally inedible.

Admittedly, not everybody has a grandmother like Biddy McGrath, and probably very few have been forced to eat or drink things that they found horrible to the taste. But we must remember that out there somewhere there are still parents and grandparents whose outlook on cooking and serving food certainly differs from the norm.

Because of their industry in the kitchen, ladies tend to take much of the blame when it comes to falling short in the culinary department. You've only to listen to the average macho male conversation in the bar to appreciate the problem.

'My wife can't cook – burns salad – takes four hours to make instant coffee.'

'That's nothing, my wife tries to make chips with Smash. She bought some peas and on the packet it said 'boil separately'. Four hours we waited for those peas ... and another thing ...' etc, etc, ad nauseam.

Why? Why blame the ladies when the men are as much, if not more, at fault? Ask any male who has cooked for himself and is prepared to tell the truth and he will agree that disasters are more regular and more calamitous when a man is at the helm.

'You're limping, Charlie. Don't tell me. You had a tin of steak and kidney pudding that said "stand in boiling water" and you've scalded your feet.'

'Ha, flippin' ha,' retorted Charlie, 'you couldn't be more wrong. The limp is from being peppered with butter beans ricocheting off the ceiling after leaving the pressure cooker at the speed of bullets. Still, I've managed to make plates obsolete by eating meals direct from whichever part of the room they land.'

Yes, it's easy to raise a laugh at another's expense, but if truth were known, we've all witnessed the same and worse. Take Auntie Marcella. A fine Irish lady, sister of my wife's mother and cook extraordinaire. Raised in the belief that 'all meals are good if they're a lot', – Marcella spent her life *almost* getting meals right. ' 'Tis easy,' said she, 'in the oven I puts a big piece of meat and a little piece of meat. When the little one's burnt, the big one's ready.'

A simple, but sure method, true. As was her gathering of ingredients. She gave me a list for the supermarket once and it read, 'Butter, eggs, trees.'

'Trees, Auntie?' I inquired.

'Sure I can't spell broccoli,' she smiled. And I smiled. But then, of course, that was before she made the onion sauce. What a sauce that was. Cooked for seven of us, including the four children, it had all the appearance of a perfect creation, but tasted a little odd. Nobody was keen to eat it, so as head of the family I ate virtually all of it.

'You kids will never grow big and strong if you don't eat up all your grub,' I said smugly.

Next morning found me a little less than smug when Pat confessed that she couldn't find the daffodil bulbs she'd been meaning to plant and that it was obvious that Auntie had cooked them. For several hours they'd not had the nerve to tell me. Instead, they'd followed me around, constantly asking me if I felt all right, while checking my cranium for any growth.

An odd story but perfectly true. So who's to say that there aren't truthful origins to other tales? Could it be that a lady once asked a butcher for a humped-backed rabbit because she wanted to make a rabbit pie and couldn't get the dough to rise? Was it she who rounded on her husband and said he'd have to wait a little longer for the pie because she hadn't finished plucking the rabbit? If so, she could have been the lady who bought a three-foot-long dessert tray because she was making a rhubarb pie...

Whichever way you look at home cooking, the pointers are that eating out is much more preferable.

'Your meal's a bit of a mixture. The chips caught fire and fell into the trifle and I had to pour the soup over them to put them out.'

'She's an odd character. Won't use tea bags. She says by the time you've cut the corners off you might as well have used loose tea. We went to their house for Christmas dinner. We complained that the turkey tasted funny and she explained, "The poor thing got burned so I rubbed some Vaseline on it." '

Ah, the joys of home cooking. Always your favourite meal served in your favourite way, at the most convenient time. Well, almost:

'This steak's burned to a crisp.'

'I know. You asked for it cooked like mother used to make and she always burned it.'

Ah yes, mother.

Wasn't it mother who always insisted that we eat our carrots so that we'd be able to see in the dark? Wasn't it mother who made us eat our crusts of bread to make our hair curly? Presumably, mothers worldwide were trying to build a race of fuzzy-headed people with perfect night sight, but what for? Whatever the reason, the new order would have to be healthy and immune to coughs and colds. This of course meant being plied with the essence of all goodness – castor oil. How devious this liquid made parents in their desperate efforts to make us partake of it: 'Every time you swallow a teaspoonful I'll put a shiny penny in the big red money box on the mantelpiece.' Little did I know that when the box was full, Dad used the money to buy another bottle of castor oil.

Oh how cruel can be the ways of adults when they think it is for the overall good. Take the tale of the not-so-well-off family seated at the table for Christmas dinner, and young Arthur says, 'Hey Dad. This turkey tastes funny, and has anybody seen Harry my rabbit?'

Silence.

'I'm just saying, Dad. This turkey tastes funny and has anybody seen Harry my rabbit?'

Silence.

Suddenly light dawns, and Arthur continues. 'Hey Dad. We're not eating Harry are we?'

'No, no,' replied the father, 'we're eating a duck, and it was a naughty duck. It ate Harry.'

Sad, maybe. True, probably not. But certainly typical of some of the odder tales relating to food and eating. For every story of gastronomic delight there are at least a dozen of gastronomic woe.

'I'm not saying her cooking was bad, but I broke a tooth on the gravy.'

Then of course there are the apocryphal stories that always happened to a 'bloke in the pub' or 'a friend of the sister-in-law'. You know the ones.

The bloke has been home for lunch, and has just left for the office when his wife sees the cat staggering into the kitchen.

'My God,' she thinks. 'It has just finished eating the scraps off my husband's plate! Could it be that the food was off?'

Just then the cat retches, heaves, gags for breath, rolls its eyes and falls into a deathlike faint. In a total panic, the lady rings the emergency services and begs them to hurry to the aid of her poisoned husband.

Squeals of tyres, much clattering of feet and extremely garbled explanations followed as ambulance men bundled hubby into the vehicle and began pumping his stomach – not the world's most wonderful experience. Two hours later, and hubby is semi-comfortable in a hospital ward, still under observation and taking 'nil by mouth'.

Now comes the twist in the tale. Worried wife opens the door to a distressed window cleaner who is sorry to disturb her but was just inquiring about the cat's condition.

'You see, as I was driving away at lunchtime, the cat ran under the wheels of my van. I knew I hit it quite hard, but then it staggered away and I thought it was only winded.'

Better safe than sorry I suppose – but try explaining that to the man in hospital. Although, were he to pause a little and think of how he could have felt were the lady's fears justified, he might be more forgiving: let's face it, we've all at some time regretted certain food or drink we've taken. There's always someone who goes out on the town, drinks ten pints of Guinness, twelve large whiskies, two Green Goddesses and then goes through the entire menu at an Indian restaurant. At five in the morning, he's the one on his knees in the bathroom vowing, 'Never again' and explaining, 'I must have eaten a bad prawn.'

There's nothing more uncomfortable than an upset stomach. It's bad enough when a germ is to blame. But self-inflicted illness has got to be the worst. To start with, nobody has any sympathy for you and can't wait to say things like:

'Should have taken more water with it.'
'You need a hair of the dog.'
'When will you ever learn?'

The world is full of people who can't wait to ridicule your condition, or worse still, offer their own helpful advice on how to cure your ailment.

Personally, I've never found the perfect antidote to bad eating or over-imbibing. One that came near was a concoction invented by a babysitter we once had. Monica was a nineteen year old who used to help out at functions where her father provided the catering. She wouldn't drink till the end of the evening, by which time there would be little to mix with the spirits. So she would have whisky and blackcurrant or gin and ginger or some other devilish brew.

To recover her spirits from such an intake she would pour a bottle of tomato juice into a pint of lager and quaff the lot in one swallow. For me, the *sight* of the remedy was enough to have me retching.

'It's kill or cure,' Monica used to say. It must be a cure; she's still alive. And so are we. Because for all the oddball stories we may hear, there's no disguising the fact that food and drink are good for us – especially when taken in moderation. Even in times of the direst poverty, it's amazing how home cooking can still provide sustenance. In my own time, I've witnessed minor miracles in the kitchen.

Take Scouse. Scouse, or to be more exact Lob Scouse, is a Liverpool dish quite similar to Irish Stew. It dates back to the hard times and consists of any and every vegetable and meat that can be lobbed into a continuously boiling pot. Pearl barley, beans, bones, all can be added and simmered for ever to glean the goodness.

'Scouse isn't cooked, there's no recipe, it just accumulates!' is a well-known Merseyside adage. What it does add is that the heavenly potion is full of nourishment and puts a skin on your back like velvet.

I've loved Scouse, or stews of any kind since childhood. They're fairly easy and really cheap to produce, easy to digest and very filling. Youngsters today would be amazed at the value of eating this type of meal, senior citizens regrettably often have to rely on it. It's difficult not to dwell on the old days and hard times but sometimes there's no harm in thinking back:

'When I was young, we were so poor, the first time I saw a butcher's shop I thought there'd been an accident.'

'You could always tell the posh people. They made bread puddings with Hovis.'

'I came from a deprived area. We had a nice house – semi-condemned. People wiped their feet coming out. The walls of our house were so thin, we once opened the oven door and caught the bloke next door dipping his bread in our gravy.'

Every generation could look back and embellish the facts. But in my own case, I prefer to reflect on the old days with pride. I liked powdered eggs, a delicacy sent in tins from the United States and pure magic in the hands of my mum and Auntie May.

In fact, it was two years after the war before I discovered that there was such a thing as a boiled or fried egg – I couldn't believe they had yolks. It was around this time that I learned that there was meat to be bought in the butcher's shop. Steaks, chops, rashers of bacon – these were like the wonders of Aladdin's Cave. Not surprising when your wartime diet centred around pigs' trotters, neck end of lamb, knuckles of beef and ox tails.

One day I must ask my old school mates what they thought animals consisted of. My own opinion was that they were a mass of bones with slivers of meat hanging off. And all covered in hide to hold it all together. It's a bit like the first time my wife Pat came home saying she'd bought some boneless chicken legs. She really meant those delicacies which have only a wee bone among all the flesh. But to my mind's eye it brought a picture of huge wobbly birds slithering around on the farmyard trying to stand up.

Strange how this chapter began as a comic look at home cooking and has now degenerated into a bizarre examination of people's mental approach to food and feeding. It just shows how important we regard eating; the need for food often transcends all other needs. Take the classic tale of the lady who opened the front door in tears.

'My God, Betty what's wrong?' inquired her neighbour.

'It's Frank,' she sobbed. 'He went down the garden this morning to pick some cabbages for lunch. He suddenly keeled over and died from a heart attack.'

'Oh no, Betty, whatever did you do?' asked the neighbour.

'We had to open a tin of peas,' was the reply.

Priorities are priorities no matter what, and even no matter the cost. I remember when Pat decided to 'cut out the big boys' and make her own ice-cream.

'Ideal,' said she, 'for when the grandchildren come round, and so much cheaper than store-bought stuff.'

It made sense but then I was only half-listening while watching the snooker. Somehow the initial outlay passed me by – an arm, a leg and a lung seems to be the going price for the equipment, and that's without the ingredients. And nobody mentions the time consumed in learning the do's and don'ts of iced confectionery.

The nightmare began when the actual machine arrived and it was not already assembled. This took best part of an afternoon and evening, notwithstanding the fact that there was no three-point plug included, a fact that wasn't noticed until all the local electrical stores were closed. We solved that one by finding a hair dryer that nobody was using and performing a transplant. Then, after long discussions and reading and re-reading of instructions, we agreed on the way the whole thing should be assembled. The actual assembling proved a poser because the thing began to spread in size as various bits were added, a little like the Lego set from hell. Soon an entire section of kitchen unit top was taken up with this mechanical overload and pots, pans, toasters and microwaves were being shifted around into odd corners from which some have still not returned. At last the thing was complete and screwed and bolted together. Ingredients were gathered in its presence and all was set for the morrow and the wondrous creation of ice-cream to rival the world's best. In faith, our kitchen looked like a mini factory – wires, pipes, pieces of machinery of differing sizes. Surely Wall's or Lyons Maid had no larger areas of production?

All was still that evening while the house slept, safe in the knowledge that on the morrow the womenfolk would be hard at it creating the sweet delight for which father had doled out a month's wages.

'You stay in bed and have a rest, Dad,' suggested one.

'We'll wake you with a thumping great bowl full of ice-cream for breakfast,' added another.

'I'll slip out of bed about seven o'clock,' said Pat. 'You won't hear me get up.'

And I didn't. No, truthfully, at seven o'clock I did not notice Pat rising. Nor at ten minutes past did I hear her descend the stairs and switch on the contraption newly assembled in the kitchen. No. I can honestly say I slept through those first twelve minutes – it was the three hours that followed that ruined my day. Once the ingredients were added and the machine switched to 'on' the noise started and never stopped. Mingling with the tortured sound of cogs and wheels grinding at wrong speeds in opposite directions and metal and plastic being wrenched and shuddered out of place, were the high-pitched, almost shrieking voices of the O'Connor ladies as they each tried to disown the very obvious cock-ups being made.

'Too much sugar,' screamed one.

'That's your fault,' said a second. 'I told you to weigh it all out.'

'Mind that hose at the end,' screeched a third.

'Look it's spraying stuff everywhere.'

'Don't just stand there. Switch it off.'

'Switch what off?'

'Too late.'

'Too late for what?'

'Be quiet or you'll wake the whole house.'

'Yes, be quiet or they'll think we can't cope.'

'Well, we can't can we?'

And they couldn't. After twenty of the longest minutes in household history, I rose and wandered casually downstairs as if I'd heard nothing. The scene was like something out of *Alien II*. Mess? You've seen nothing like it, powder, sugar, stodgy lumps of what looked like stale plasticine, uncoupled hoses, lidless plastic containers weeping slimy contents – it was horrible.

'How's it going?' I ventured bravely.

'Not bad,' said Pat. Not bad? My God, I thought, I've seen bad and this is bad – no, *this* is worse.

'Would you like to try some?' asked Helen, our youngest. I did. I sampled the sum total of all they had produced. The entire crop from that day's crashing, banging and screaming. It all fitted on half a dessertspoon and tasted like cold custard with chalk in it. I swallowed it manfully and smiled a queerish smile of satisfaction. 'Mmm,' I said but didn't mean it. 'Anyway, well done, but I must get on with some paperwork.'

I ambled into the lounge, leaving the growing argument as to who was going to wash up. That's when I realized that each individual part had to be hand cleaned – no uniform bits to go in a dishwasher – all to be done the hard way. That's also when I realized that this whole adventure would never, ever be repeated in our house – and it hasn't. In fact it's that long ago since that awesome day, and the machinery has been lying in the garage so long that their memories of it are already fading. On several occasions, even those who were present at the disaster have looked at the mass of rubber, metal and plastic and said, 'I wonder what that is?'

They should ask me. I remember. I'll never forget. Next to the outfits that each of my womenfolk wore to my daughter Frances's wedding, that machine is the most expensive thing I've ever bought that was only used once...

8

To Try It
You've Got To Buy It

It seems that virtually every conversation, no matter what the topic, eventually gets round to food or drink. We even use it in describing human behaviour:

'They're very posh, them next door. You know the type, grapes on the sideboard and nobody sick.'

We can't escape references in general conversation because anything so vital to our well-being also provides a common bond. It's a bit like talking about the weather – at least it's something we can agree to disagree about. I mean, who'd be a weather man or woman? Someone is alleged to have proved (a bit like a story from a mate of someone's father down the pub) that the weather people get fifty-one per cent of their predictions wrong. Therefore, it follows, according to this person, that if they forecast the total opposite of what they believe, they'd be more accurate – yes, and as

I've said before, if you believe that one I've got a bridge to sell you. But who'd be a weather person? And for that matter – who'd be a shopkeeper? Who is masochistic enough to stand for the daily bombardment to the senses that only the public can deliver? And when it comes to foodstuffs it's always going to be 'advantage customer'.

For years I opened my act with a story dedicated to the ladies present. I did it to prove how shrewd and sensible the lasses were and, in doing so, forced the gentlemen present, albeit grudgingly, to agree that they were married to the more brilliant sex.

The tale is of the lady who went into the grocer's store and asked for some ham. 'I want some ham,' said she, 'but I don't want the packet stuff. Get that big piece there and put it on the slicer.'

The grocer staggered under the weight of a full side of ham, flopped it on the slicer and began to carve.

Slice, slice, slice, slice – pause.

'Having a party?' he inquired.

'Listen, nosy, just keep slicing,' said the customer.

Slice, slice, slice – pause.

'Kid's birthday or something?' he smiled.

'I've told you once,' she glowered, 'keep slicing.'

Slice, slice, slice – then –

'OK, stop,' said the lady. 'Now, the next two slices I'll have.'

Isn't shopping for food just made for banter? Isn't it really half the reason we still visit butchers' shops as opposed to grabbing plastic covered portions off refrigerated shelves?

'Excuse me, butcher, there's a sausage on the floor.'

'It's all right, I've got my foot on it.'

I like that line.

I also like the story of the smart alec who asked for a

yard of pork and the butcher gave him three pig's feet.
There are so many of them aren't there?

'I'd like two pounds of bacon and can you make it
lean?'
'Certainly, madam, in which direction?'

'Have you got pig's feet?'
'Yes, madam.'
'Well, trot over there and get me some sausages.'

There are some legendary tales which must at some
time have had a foundation in truth. Take the man who
went into the butcher's shop accompanied by a huge
Alsatian. Quick as a flash the beast leaped over the
counter, grabbed a massive joint of beef in its jaws and
bolted out of the establishment.

'Is that your dog?' roared the proprietor.

'It used to be,' said the customer, 'but it fends for
itself now.'

Then there was the story, much-used by comedians,
and afterwards claimed to be 'a true story that
happened to me' of the lady who went to her local meat
shop to complain.

'Last week I bought a leg of lamb here. It cost a lot of
money. Best quality, you said,' she grumbled, 'no
additives, just pure lamb, you said – feed a dozen, you
said. Well, let me tell you. I put that leg in the oven and
when it came out it had shrunk to half its size.'

'That's funny,' smiled the butcher, 'I had a similar
experience myself. Last week I bought a sweater, pure
wool, the man said. Last a lifetime, the man said. Great
value, the man said. Two days later I put it in the
washing machine and when it came out it had shrunk
to half the size. It must have come off the same sheep.'

You can't invent stuff like that can you? Where else but face to face with the public would you hear the likes?

'My Mum said could she have a sheep's head, oh and by the way, could you leave the legs on?'

It almost seems to be the butchers' lot to suffer the slings and arrows of cheap humour and cruel gibes, so its good to hear of them retaliating. Do you recall the tale of the man of meat who was bartering with the local pet shop over the price of a budgerigar?

'You've got to remember that this is a very talented bird,' said the owner.

'I agree,' said the butcher, 'but I think you're charging just a little too much.'

'So make me an offer,' smiled the budgie keeper.

'Tell you what,' suggested the butcher, 'what about I pay you the same as I charged for my prime turkeys at Christmas?'

'It's a deal,' said the pet shop man.

'Good,' grinned our hero, 'because for the turkeys I was charging £2 a pound – what's the weight of this bird?'

I'm immediately reminded of a couple of turkey tales. One was about the farmer who managed, after twenty years of trying, to rear a breed of turkey with six legs. He figured that as everyone liked turkey legs it would be a big sales grabber at Christmas.

'What did the legs taste like?' asked a friend.

'I don't know,' moaned the farmer, 'I've never been able to catch one of them.'

Then there was the story of the skinflint farmer who wrote to his niece:

'I was going to send you a turkey for Christmas but it got better.'

But before we get too involved with tales of turkeys

and meat, let's spare a thought for the other sufferers. What about the fish trade?

'Can I have a pair of kippers please?'
'We haven't got a pair left.'
'Well give me two odd ones. She won't know the difference.'

'Are those fish fresh?'
'Fresh? They're lying on top of each other.'

'Can I have a cod's head for the cat?'
'Why, are you doing a transplant?'

You see, you don't get a lot of that cross talk when picking up items from a shelf do you? And before I pay due respect to supermarkets, let me just ponder on some events that could only happen at 'we serve you' venues.
'Are these oranges from Israel?'
'Why, are you going to talk to them or eat them?'
Great comeback from the supreme banter merchant, the barrow trader:

'You said these apples were five for a pound. There's only four in this bag.'
   'Yes, love, one of them was bad so I threw it away for you.'

'Three pork chops and can you cut the fat off.'
'They don't peel bananas before they weigh them you know.'

'Can I have two ounces of corned beef please.'
'Any invitations to the party, pal?'

Do those lines just come out naturally, or is there a

handbook that we don't know about called *How to Flatten Every Query*? Maybe there is. Maybe we should all subscribe. Think of the fun, or not, that we'd have:

Wife – 'Can you put the kettle on, dear?'

Husband – 'No, I can't get my arm through the spout.'

Funny? Maybe. Injurious to the husband's health? Certainly.

Perhaps the greatest butt of any joke has to be the American tourist. It seems that worldwide, he or she is the one target that all put-downs are aimed at. I suppose it must be the condescending way they speak. Take,

for example, the lady selling fruit and veg from a barrow in a Liverpool High Street. A rather large Texan approached and began checking out the goods.

'What are they?' he asked, pointing at the Golden Delicious.

'Apples, dear – £1 a pound,' smiled the lady.

'Apples? You call them apples? Why in my country we have apples ten times that size. And what are they?' he inquired pointing again.

'Oranges,' snapped Miss Nose-Out-Of-Joint.

'Oranges? *Oranges*? Why in Texas we've got orange pips bigger than those things.'

As he spoke he picked up a rather large cabbage.

'And before you say another word,' said the barrow lady, 'put that brussels sprout down if you're not going to buy it.'

Mind you, as funny as we are with other people, on the subject of food and beverages, we're even harder on ourselves. I recall working at a well known holiday centre and opening the act with the usual 'Are you enjoying yourselves – any complaints?' Normally this gets a positive 'we're having a great time' response. But not this time. This particular night I got:

'I've got a complaint,' from a rather large chap in the front row.

'Pardon?'

'I've got a complaint. The food is rubbish,' he bellowed.

'It's what?'

'The food is rubbish. Worst I've ever tasted,' he insisted.

'Why didn't you go self-catering?' I asked.

'We did,' he replied, to gales of laughter.

It reminded me of the workmen on the building site who constantly moaned to each about the sandwiches they brought to work.

'I've got ham again,' said Charlie. 'I'm going to have to have a serious word with the missus about this.'

'And me,' said Mike. 'My missus keeps giving me cheese. I'm going to tell her to change her tune.'

'It's all right for you,' said Paddy. 'I get tuna every day, but what can I do? I live on my own.'

But would complaining ever solve the problem? Well, there are different schools of thought on this one. The first school believe, and I think I agree, that no matter how a person reacts to a complaint the moaner seems never to be satisfied.

Take the roadworker who constantly complained, not of the quality of his sandwiches, but the quantity.

'Only two slices yesterday. Only two slices,' he grumbled. Long suffering wifey applied herself a little harder and improved the amount.

'Only four slices today. Just four slices. What's a man supposed to do on just four slices?'

Next day, the lass doubled the dose and still he complained.

Finally, she could take it no longer. She bought a huge loaf, sliced it across the middle and stuffed it with ham, eggs and salad. Hubby arrived home at six and said, calm as you like,

'I see we're back to two slices again.' Men!

That story's as bad as the conversation in the pub between two hard-done-by husbands. (Isn't it amazing how well these guys look despite their grumblings?)

'I don't know about you, but I'm sick to death of the carry out my wife keeps giving me. I'm going to have it out with her when I get home,' said one.

'Be careful,' cautioned the other, 'I complained about my lunchbox the other day and the wife gave me KiteKat sandwiches for revenge. Mind you, I got my own back. I had her up all night looking for mice.'

All well and good, these anecdotes, but what a lot of husbands do not realize, until they try it, is the difficulty found in shopping for variety these days. Probably the answer has to be the supermarket where, in theory, all is displayed for your delectation and nothing could be quicker or easier. Oh yeah?

To begin with we must accept various truths regarding these emporiums. Supermarkets are places where you can find anything but the children. Have you spent the best part of a Saturday morning racing up and down aisles looking for a five year old? It got so bad with our lot, that I used to insist that they wore vivid yellow shirts or jumpers to make them stand out.

The next problem is that, on a very busy day, and most days are busy, you can never find anybody to direct you to the counter you want. I mean, wouldn't you think they'd put the breakfast cereals near the bacon and eggs? Or am I just being picky? Why aren't the beans near the bread? You know, beans on toast? Why should the soup be where the tinned fruit is and not where the tuna and crab is? Why is it that every shelf, and I mean every shelf, in the whole place has sweets and chocolates on the lower levels? Who hasn't arrived at the till with at least a couple of youngsters hanging onto their clothes and a hundredweight of goodies that they've lobbed into their trolley.

And you think that is bad enough? Why, your problems are only just beginning. The fun really starts in a supermarket when you try to get out. Theoretically it is a simple process. Whatever number of shoppers there may be, there are at least as many checkout points. This is true, but how many times have you seen them all manned at the same time? Better still, how many times have you seen them manned at all? Usually the entire checkout force consists of one little old lady, or a trainee, who can hardly work the till and doesn't know the price of anything. And aren't you always the one who picks up an item without a price on it? Isn't it you who always sparks off that big electronic booming voice, 'Customer checkout please.'

All right, it is getting better. In a lot of places they now have a quick checkout service bay for those who've six items or fewer. That's quite an interesting place to hang around. It's surprising how many people can't count to six, and you'd be amazed at the bouts of fisticuffs this can cause. Pushing, shoving, bellowing, muttering – it's like Question Time in the House of Commons. To be fair to the customer, there is nothing more infuriating than a quick service that isn't. It seems that we're constantly at the mercy of the system, but what can we do? Well, we could rebel, provided we all kept our heads and worked together. Without warning, one day we should all hit the supermarkets at the same time, load a trolley each – I mean to overflowing – and take them to the checkouts and just leave them there. What a commotion that would cause. By Jove that would liven up some ideas. Cruel? Yes. Unfair? Probably.

Remember, the art of buying and selling is just a part of a much larger overall plan which begins with the food producer and only ends when we've eaten the darned stuff. All the way down the line there are hard-working people whose efforts must be rewarded and whose feelings must be respected. Also there are problems of storage, transport, delivery and replenishment. And most importantly, there are problems with the advertising and promotion of items. I mean they don't just appear to us as if in a dream. Someone, somewhere has to spend an awful lot of time and energy in tickling our fancies and pushing forward the various new lines.

Pat's late Aunt Marcella was an avid follower of TV advertising and in the end could only ask for products by quoting the various jingles. The actual brand names were forgotten in the blurb and the hype of the on-screen bombardment. Often she would totally confound shopkeepers and supermarket staff by literally re-enacting the entire commercial in order to make herself understood.

'I hope she never needs laxatives or haemorrhoid cream,' said Pat's dad wryly.

But it is a fact, is it not, that the more we poor shoppers are hammered by the big sell, the more we get confused as to what is best for us to buy. Eventually, I have to admit, I tend to give up and just grab the nearest to what I want and make a swiftish exit. There was a time in our hungry years, when a school teacher's pay was all that kept us from starvation, when I would tread aisles looking for a money-saving snip or a cheap substitute for what I really wanted. Nowadays it seems that price doesn't always determine quality, and the reasons for goods being on special offer are beyond comprehension. 'Loss leader' is a wonderful phrase.

Apparently it means that a certain item is offered at a ridiculously low price just to get you into the store. It always reminds me of the two shops in the same street who started a battle of 'loss leaders'. The first day, one displayed a banner proclaiming 'Baked Beans – now only 50p per tin'.

The next day the other had a sign saying, 'Baked Beans here only 25p per tin'. 'Next day shop one replied with 'Baked Beans 15p per tin'.

Next day came the ultimate challenge, 'Baked beans, 2p per tin'.

That was too much for the first shopkeeper who stormed round to his competitor in high dudgeon and said, 'You're mad, totally mad. There's no possible way you can sell beans at 2p per tin and make a profit. In fact you'd be making a massive loss.'

'It doesn't worry me,' said his opposite number, 'we don't sell beans anyway.'

You don't think that's a logical argument? Let me quote you one even more bizarre. I refer to the tale of the man who went to a store and asked for some grapes.

'Yessir. We have some beautiful grapes and they're £1 a pound,' smiled the proprietor.

'That's very dear,' said the customer, 'the shop in the high street only charges 75p per pound.'

'Well,' said the owner, 'why didn't you get them there?'

'Oh, you see,' said the customer, 'they didn't have any left.'

'Well,' beamed the shopkeeper, 'when we haven't any left ours are 75p per pound as well.'

'Right,' said the customer, 'I'll come back when you haven't any left.'

Who knows if that reasoning spurs us to do things

totally out of character. I recall a piece I read once about the little general store in the wilds of the Yukon during the gold rush days. A miner came in, looked around and was amazed to see every shelf, every cupboard and all the floor space crammed with packets of salt.

'By gosh,' he said to the storekeeper, 'you must sell some salt.'

'On the contrary,' replied the man, 'I sell hardly any. But the man who sells *me* salt, boy, can he sell salt.'

Proof, I suppose, of the powers of persuasion that can be brought to bear on the weak willed and, let's face it, the not so weak willed. Apparently there is a legendary story that is quoted to all courses in the advertising training trade regarding the sale of salmon. It seems that a small fishing village on the east coast of America was having major financial difficulties. Their only catch seemed to be white salmon and there didn't appear to be a great demand for it. What to do? Well the townsfolk agreed to invest what little resources they had in employing a high-flying New York firm to take charge of their advertising. Surprisingly, the firm's top brainbox agreed to think about the problem overnight and came up with a solution. This he duly did, and what a solution! He gave them the all-time classic slogan to go on the labels on the tins and it said:

'Genuine white salmon. Guaranteed not to go red in the tin.'

Instant success, sales soared, the village prospered, and red salmon dealers couldn't sue. After all, what did the slogan say that was derogatory?

But buying and selling will always lead to problems because human nature is involved and no two people are totally alike. The classic line – 'one man's meat is another man's poison' is one of the most true of all home truths and how we prove that every day. I'm sure

if the Almighty could have a second go at sending us beatitudes (you know the ones – 'Blessed are the meek for they shall inherit the earth'), he'd have given us:

'Blessed are they that are easily satisfied, for they shall be loudly proclaimed throughout the shopping mall.'

For surely what pleases one is sure to displease another; what seems ambrosia to Peter can be anathema to Paul. Even a sweet tooth can be soured by too much of a good thing. I've seen that at first hand and I am a witness. We were working on a brand new television show on Thames TV and, as is almost the norm, it was of American origin. The producer of the original series in New York came over to lend us his expertise and experience, and glad we were of it. At lunch on the first day we regaled him with the finest salads, fish and cold meats all of which he nibbled and poked at but hardly swallowed. Just at the point when I was convinced he had a dietary problem he spotted the dessert menu.

'Gee you've got apple pie,' he enthused.

'Yes, sir,' said the waitress, 'and what would you like with it? We've got custard, dairy cream and ice-cream.'

'Yes,' was all he said.

'Yes?' queried the young lady.

'Yes,' he smiled, 'all of them.'

And he ate the lot. A possible zillion calories on one plate – yuk! It looked like something out of the *Quatermass* film. It probably tasted sickly, sickly sweet. But he threw it down with relish and followed it with After Eight Mints – at 2 pm!. The joke was that during the course of the meal he had been bemoaning his health. He'd had major heart problems requiring a bypass.

'Can't believe it's happening to me. Must be something hereditary.' Sure, pal, sure. If you believe that, you can plait soot, or nail jelly to the ceiling.

By the by ... Back to buying and selling and a gentle

little chuckle to round off. Ostensibly the story is of the rather hen-pecked-looking chap who was sheepishly wandering round the lingerie area of a department store.

'Can I help you sir?' called an approaching assistant.

Going bright red from toes to forehead, the customer spluttered, 'I ... I ... I'm looking for a new bra for my wife as a surprise for her birthday.'

'Very nice, sir, and what size would she be?'

'That's the trouble,' explained the embarrassed one, 'I don't know. Haven't a clue.'

'Well, what do her boobs look like – melons?'

'Oh no,' said the little fellow.

'Pineapples?'

'No.'

'Apples?'

'Er, no.'

'Eggs?'

'Yes,' he sighed, 'they're like eggs – only fried.'

9

Eating and Drinking Around the World and Elsewhere

'This coffee is imported all the way from South America,' said one old dear in the café.

'Good heavens,' remarked her friend, 'and it's still warm.'

Ah, the innocence of it all. But isn't it the same innocence we all show when confronted with conditions and customs of other places? Doesn't it apply even more so when confronting strange food and beverages? Gives a new meaning or postscript to tried and trusted sayings like, 'It's a small world – but I wouldn't like to eat my way round it.'

You've hardly got to leave your home town to appreciate the difference in recipes and delicacies. From Scouse in Liverpool, it's hardly a stone's throw to Lancashire hot pot in Wigan, and not all that far from Yorkshire pudding in Bradford. Moving up the map we find stottie cake in the north-east. (Stottie cake is difficult to define, God knows how hard it is to prepare), followed by the delights of Bonnie Scotland – haggis, porridge, oat cakes and the like – and of course the very best whiskies in the world.

Just as an aside, I thought I'd re-tell that lovely story of St Peter talking to God with reference to the land of the heather.

'Indeed, Lord,' said he, 'you have saved the best in all the world for the people they call the Scots. The best mountains, the best glens, the best rivers, the finest of whiskies. Why give it all to one small nation?'

'Well,' beamed the Almighty. 'It's the least I could do when you see the neighbours I've lumbered them with.'

So the Scots are multi-blessed and therefore we should start with them when looking at food and drink on a world scale. I thought maybe we could begin with a story that not only is true, but also encapsulates the quick wit of the Celts along with the little failing that some of them have – meanness. No, I'm not referring to the recipe for an Aberdeen omelette that starts, 'first borrow two eggs ...' No indeed. This story was told to me by the legendary Scottish comic, Chick Murray, and refers to the famous country dance band leader, Jimmy Shand. Apparently Jimmy and his five-piece band were on a tour of the Highlands and Islands of Scotland. They were staying overnight in a wee guest house run by a very dour-looking lady with a bun in her hair tied back so tight that her eyes slanted orientally. The boys had a peaceful night's sleep and in the morning they repaired to the dining room for breakfast. There on the table were six cups of tea, no pot, six slices of toast, no butter, and one tiny, *tiny* pot of honey. Jimmy took one look at the latter and remarked to the lady, 'I see you keep a bee.'

You know, I know exactly how he felt. I've had similar, never worse, but similar. It seems to be the lot of travelling people to meet the oddities of life. Any sales folk reading this will, I'm sure, agree that there's nowt queerer than folk. Certainly in the showbusiness fraternity there are basic rules of thumb for theatrical digs. Number one – never stay in a place that has a fat dog – the food is obviously so bad that it gets more than its share. Always beware of the lady of the house – generally speaking she is a law unto herself. The late Les Dawson always affirmed that:

'You could tell by looking at her what was in store for meals. If she only had one stocking on, then it was jam roly poly.' Disgusting.

On another occasion he complained: 'Sometimes we got windmill pudding, so called because if the wind blew your way you got a bit.'

Probably these are exaggerations. In fact, knowing Les, they are definite exaggerations. But just occasionally they do get near the truth. I'm reminded of a lovely anecdote told to me by Arthur Askey. In the immediate post-war days everything was scarce, and everything – bread, meat, eggs, sweets and so on – was rationed. Arthur had been asked to do a favour by opening a garden fête organized by the local butcher. In return he was given a two-pound chunk of best steak – a king's ransom couldn't have bought it. Returning to his digs, he asked the landlady if she would cook it for his evening meal.

'Certainly, Mr Askey,' she said.

'And will you boil it?' asked Arthur.

'Yes,' she replied.

'I bloody thought you would,' muttered the little fellow.

So spoke the long-suffering voice of experience.

Too often and too long have entertainers undergone the slings and arrows, that it becomes second nature to cover one's back. Dora Bryan tells the tale of harder times when, in a similar situation to Arthur's, a favour was repaid with the gift of some new potatoes – a delicacy. Her landlady was delighted to be asked to cook them.

'Shall I mash them to go with the sausage?' she asked sweetly.

'No, no,' said Dora, 'just boil them. I want to make sure I get the same number back that I started with.'

Aha, what logic.

Before we launch ourselves fully into the myths and legends surrounding eating away, maybe I should throw in my own small encounter with strange domiciles and unusual cooks. I was touring the nightclubs and working-men's club circuit of Great Britain and for six weeks I was based in Newcastle. It was the mid-sixties and the world was buzzing with the Mersey Sound, Mini cars and mini skirts. Americans were making a sort of pilgrimage to Britain to find out what was new and everyone seemed to have money to burn. I was lucky to find accommodation in one of the finest theatrical residences in the north-east – Roker House, Sunderland. The boss lady was a lovely person and her cooking was second to none. In her own special way she made all and sundry welcome and made sure that nobody was ever embarrassed. There was never a pork or bacon dish served, lest Jewish folk were offended. And on Fridays, just for the Catholics, no meat was served. Roker House was a house for theatrical turns and the charges were most reasonable. I suppose it's easy in times like those when the head spins with happiness and contentment, to gradually let the guard slip and fall into wrong ways.

It was like this. Christmas was upon us and the few entertainers who were staying up for the festivities were asked a special favour by our hostess.

'Christmas Day, boys. If it's not too much trouble I'd ask you to look after yourselves. There's plenty of food, bread, milk and so on. The turkey and all the trimmings will be put in the oven and you can tuck in at your own convenience. All I'm asking is that you serve yourselves and, if it's not too much trouble, wash up afterwards.'

Who could resist such a charming request from such a charming lass? Eight of us, hard-bitten comics, singers, dancers and jugglers settled down to do a little self-catering, or at least self-serving. No problem, easy job, no worries. Well, OK, maybe just the one. In our midst we were delighted, in fact thrilled, to have that brilliant singer, impressionist, comedian – Wee Willie Harris. For those who don't remember the little genius, it was he of the multi-coloured, dazzling hair do's and lunatic cavortings on stage and television. Easily outranking all of us in terms of ability and fame, we allowed the great man to dictate the plan of action for Christmas.

'We should,' he said earnestly, 'at least contribute something towards this meal that is of our own making. The lady has left us turkey, vegetables, Christmas cake, Christmas pud. But I think we should add one further item just to give it our own little stamp. What about some rice pudding?'

It was agreed straightaway that the great man should proceed with the cooking and all stood back to watch him produce a huge cooking pot, insert four two-pound packets of rice, four pints of milk and place in the oven. Some time later, purely out of passing curiosity, I opened the oven door and beheld a wondrous sight. The Wee Willie pudding had heated, expanded and set into what can only be described as a marble-like substance. Too much rice and too little milk had led to a huge, concrete-textured lump. We used a saw-bladed knife to cut out one segment, added about four pints of milk and eventually ended up with a not-so-bad excuse for a dessert. The rest of the block was sawn up in various pieces and distributed among the staff of the guest house to take home and water down for themselves.

Funny on reflection I suppose but just another in a long line of showbiz tales that are never conclusively proved true or false. Take the speciality act who hit on hard times. For years the great Mario had stunned the known world with a six-minute variety show featuring a parrot doing impressions of myriad people both living and dead – Elvis, John Lennon, Michael Jackson, Margaret Thatcher. You name them, this bird could do them. It so happened that poor old Mario gradually disappeared from the cabaret scene and for several years nobody knew where he'd gone. Then out of the blue an old pal stumbled across him, half drunk, in a seedy dockside bar in some God-forsaken land.

'Mario, Mario. It's you. How have you been?' asked the friend.

'Good days and bad days,' mumbled the turn. 'Ups and downs. Same as always.'

'Still doing the bird act?' inquired the pal.

'Naa, had to give it up. I'm begging on the streets now,' was the sad reply.

'Begging? But what about the act? It was superb,' said the other. 'And where's the parrot?'

'Well,' sighed Mario, 'the truth is I hit on the worst times imaginable and I was slowly starving to death, no money, no food, no hope. And to be totally honest with you, I got so hungry I ate the parrot.'

'*Ate* the parrot?' stammered the old pal.   'How desperate you must have been. And what did the parrot taste like?'

'Turkey,' smiled Mario, 'that bird could impersonate anything.'

And you think that's bad? So do I. But here's a worse one before we move back to the plot. This is the story of the act who checked into a boarding house in Blackpool for the summer season. On being greeted by the landlady he said,

'I hope you don't mind but I do like funny breakfasts.'

'No trouble,' said the matronly lady, 'we're used to theatrical folk here. Whatever you want we can oblige.'

'I like beans,' he explained.

'No problem,' said she.

'I like lots of beans,' he went on.

'Believe me, no bother,' she retorted.

'I mean stacks of beans,' he insisted.

'Stacks it shall be,' she smiled.

So for his first morning's breakfast the guest was served four large tins of beans on toast and he ate the lot. Then, calm as you like, he wandered out of the door and on to the Golden Mile.

Two hours later a police car arrived and the constable produced a photograph, proffered it to the landlady and said, 'Do you know this man?'

'Yes,' she replied, 'he's staying here for the summer. Came yesterday. Why, what's up?'

'I'm sorry to tell you that we've found his body at the foot of Blackpool Tower,' said a serious-faced sergeant, 'and we think he's thrown himself off.'

'Well, I can't understand that,' said the matron, 'because he was full of beans when he left here.' Ouch!!

(Quickly, O'Connor, quickly get the chapter back on

track before the reader finds your address and comes round to break your windows.)

Before that bout of lunacy, I was describing the reactions we have to strange dishes and customs and, of course, strange locations. I suppose one of the most strange of places to eat is at sea. Mother Nature seems to have given us different levels of tolerance of sea travel. Some, like my wife, just adapt to the pitching and rolling as if it were an everyday occurrence. Others, like myself, have to take time to adapt. Gradually, I seem to be mastering the job. Either that, or the ships I go on are bigger and more stable, or the seas are not as choppy. However, this was not always the case and here I give salutary warning to all land lubbers who are pondering a life on the ocean wave. Always remember, through good feelings and bad, that just when you think you've got the water mastered, it sneaks up on you again. It's a paraphrase really of the line from the film, 'just when you thought it was safe to go back on the water …'

I learned my lesson the hard way, on my first-ever long sea voyage. Oh yes, in my youth I'd been afloat – the New Brighton ferry and the Royal Iris cruises on the River Mersey. But never before had I encountered the mighty sea. Pat and I paid £47 each (by God, this story is old) for a four-day 'trip to Fairyland'. Basically it was four days and three nights on a small North Sea ship going from Newcastle to Bergen and back. About eight of us were the Fairyland passengers. The others were skiers, holidaymakers or business folk who couldn't get there quick enough. Consequently, all thoughts of a cruise went straight out of the window. Instead, the captain put his head down and bombed across the main. Unused to this form of travel, my stomach rebelled and despite copious intakes of port and brandy, my spirits flagged and, instead of Fairyland, I settled for a kneeling position over the flip-up loo in our cabin. After a day and a half I found the greatest cure for sea sickness – land. Being so grateful that the lord of the waves had spared my miserable soul I went on a celebratory bash, drinking twenty something bottles of lager and going to bed that night a totally contented sailor.

Next morning the ship now moving, but still inside the confines of Bergen harbour away from large waves, I awoke and went down to the smorgasbord and break-fast. Hungry as the proverbial hunter, I got stuck into everything, making up for three lost days and the lost contents of my tummy. Scrambled eggs, bacon, sausage, ham, salami and to round it all off – curried rabbit and rice. Yes, indeed, mate, no messing about for me, not jolly Jack Tar.

This mighty meal made me a little drowsy and I chose to close my eyes, only for a few minutes, on a deckchair out in the warming sun of a Norwegian morning. What seemed like moments, but was probably an hour later I was wakened by a strange sliding feeling and a crashing noise. My eyes reacted before my stomach and I realized I was the only person on deck. The sun had gone, to be replaced by a biting wind. The ship was heaving from side to side (like my innards) and my deckchair, chained by one leg to the deck, was swirling all over the place in a force seven gale.

Gone were Pat and all the Fairylanders, each one thinking I was with the other. 'And anyway,' said my beloved later, 'you seemed to have adjusted so well that you could cope on your own.'

Would that I could. Would that I could. All right, so sea sickness is mostly in the mind. I know this. My stomach knows this too, but under pressure it's just too difficult to convince one's brain. Hard as I tried to control my feelings as I staggered from the deckchair to the nearest deck door, it was all in vain. Try as I might to think of other things like summer days and children playing, all I could recall was curried rabbit and rice and that did it. Over the side went the head, and 'Never again,' said the grey matter.

Thus I learned very early in my nautical career the truth of the old adage, 'Worse things happen at sea.' They certainly do. But so too do the funniest things happen. Over years of working on cruise liners, I've managed to glean some wonderful epics from passengers, fellow entertainers, but mostly crew. It is a source of great wonder as to what the great British public will do when their feet leave terra firma. Let me begin with an outward-bound leg of a world cruise on *QE2*. This was told to me by the actual crewman involved. He was working as a steward in one of the bars and three days out he was accosted by an elderly dowager lady, obviously on her first-ever voyage.

'Excuse me young man,' she began, 'but can you solve a mystery for me?'

'If I can, ma'am,' he smiled.

'Well,' she went on, 'I'd like to know where you go of a night.'

'Pardon?'

'Well, you don't stay on board do you?' she asked.

'Oh no, ma'am,' replied the steward with a wicked glint in his eye. 'A helicopter comes at one in the morning and takes us off and brings us back at 6.30 am.'

'I thought so,' nodded the old dear and pottered off.

Next day the same lady went to the purser's office and complained that the noise of the helicopter was keeping her awake. Funny? Yes. True? Who knows. Probably as true or false as the story of the old lass who boarded at Southampton, checked in and took her cabin keys, went for lunch and then was not seen again for two days. Eventually people began to miss her presence and reported their fears to an officer. A party of cruise staff were dispatched to her cabin and, opening the unlocked door, they found her sitting ashen-faced on her bunk.

'Thank God you've arrived,' she sobbed. 'I've been trapped here for days.'

'Trapped?' inquired a hostess. 'Trapped? But why didn't you just open the door?'

'I did,' replied the lady, 'but there's only a bathroom in there.'

'No, no, not that door,' insisted the girl. 'I meant why didn't you open *this* door?'

'Oh, I couldn't,' explained the stranded one, 'it had "do not disturb" on the handle.'

Oh well, back to the sublime and the effects that food and drink can have upon those in peril on the sea. I must confess I'm a sucker for stories of quick-thinking waiters and stewards, so let me begin with the oft-told tale of the over-busy young fellow who was bustling around the ship's restaurant serving about five tables at once. As he sped, gazelle-like, down an aisle carrying a bowl of steaming hot minestrone soup, he stumbled over the outstretched leg of an old chap who'd fallen fast asleep. In a trice, or even less, the waiter was upended and the entire contents of the bowl showered down the old boy's shirt front. As the man awoke, mumbling loudly, the re-composed waiter asked calmly, 'Do you feel better now, sir?'

I don't know how old that particular anecdote is but it came to my ears over twenty years ago and immediately inspired a cruise routine that I've used off and on ever since. Basically it involves two fictional people whom I called Pete and Pauline, much married and under travelled, who go on a world cruise to celebrate their silver-wedding anniversary. Never having been at sea before they try desperately to come to terms with the rudiments of shipboard life and come only to grief.

'Who's he?' asked Pauline of a young cabin steward. 'That bloke with the peaked cap and rings on his sleeve.'

'That,' replied the young man, 'is the purser. He's responsible for all the berths on the ship.'

'Is he?' she said. 'And he's only a little feller, isn't he?'

To celebrate their anniversary, which had been reported by family to the entertainments staff, Pete and Pauline were invited to dine at the captain's table which obviously gives a chance to use that unforgettable line: 'All the money we paid and we have to eat with the crew.'

But of course the problem with dining in style, as we all know, is what to do with what.

So it was that our second honeymooners sat at table and were faced with a battery of plates, glasses and particularly cutlery.

'We've got three knives and forks each, but don't panic,' said Pete, 'either there's three sittings or these know something that we don't. So watch them like a hawk.'

When the waiter appeared with the menu, disaster was close at hand. No one in the world has ever read a French menu quite like our hero. 'Now then, luv,' he began, to the wonder of the captain and a dozen VIPs, 'we've got a choice. There's horses dewberries, cauliflower au gratin – I think that means you get it for nothing – or minestrone soup with cretins in it. I think we'll have the soup, garston,' he smiled, 'that'll get rid of one knife and fork.'

'Now,' went on persistent Peter, further digging the hole into which he would be buried, 'the only thing I can recognize on the main course is chicken. So we'll have two of them.'

'Certainly, sir,' replied the waiter, 'and would you like *pommes de terre*?'

'No,' said Peter. 'A couple of spuds will do.'

Ah yes, when ignorance is bliss, it is folly to be wise.

But before we leave the raging main and return to earth, let me just relate a couple of my favourite maritime tales. These must go under the heading of 'I wish I'd had the nerve to do that,' and were inspired by a chance reading of an article in the London *Evening Standard*. It seems a London bus driver who had spent thirty years in the job was due to retire and on his last day at the wheel he did something he'd always longed to do. He drove round Eros three times before coming off the roundabout. Oh what I wouldn't have given to see the faces of the other motorists.

So, armed with that kind of derring do, what about the wine waiter, who shall be nameless, who was working on a cruise liner bound for Miami. At the first port of call, Madeira, he got drunk, was unable to perform his nightly duties and was subsequently fired.

'When we reach America,' said the captain, 'you will be dismissed from the company.'

Pity really that the skipper didn't wait till the man had finished work before delivering the news. Because, forget about a woman scorned, there is no more dangerous being than a waiter sacked. On the night before Miami our man was working his final shift and was serving a table full of the top customers, millionaires all, world travellers, and regular passengers on that particular liner.

'I've brought the red wine you requested, sir,' he said

to the red-faced, pompous-looking gentleman.

'Yes, yes, yes,' spluttered the man. 'But is it at room temperature?'

With that, the waiter raised the bottle to his lips, took a mighty swig, wiped his mouth with the cuff of his jacket and said, 'Yes, indeed, sir,' and began pouring it into the fellow's glass. What courage or maybe what stupidity. But what a way to go. And going out with a bang always seems more appealing than leaving with a whimper. So let's close the book on sea travel with a true story I heard while in New York.

Apparently a very famous US admiral was retiring from the service and a great dinner and ball was held in his honour. Speeches were made aplenty including one from the president himself. When it came time for the great man to reply to all the eulogies he said the same old right and trite things. 'Couldn't have done it all without my fellow officers ... blah di blah ...' Suddenly he paused, looked a little quizzical and said: 'I suppose as it's my big night I can say virtually anything I want to. So here's a thing that's been puzzling me for nigh on thirty years. In the gathering here tonight is ensign Johnson my aide since I became a flag officer, and I'd like him to answer this one question. How come in all our years on destroyers, frigates, cruisers, battleships and carriers; how come in all weathers from calm sea to hurricanes; how come in all conditions of war, under sea attack, bombing attack, submarine drill and kamikaze assaults; how come in all those situations, whenever I rang down to the galley for a mug of coffee, how come when you reached the bridge the mug was always full?'

'Well, Admiral,' said the ensign in a drawling southern voice, 'the answer is simple. When I was leaving the galley I used to take a mouthful of coffee, and just before I opened the door of the bridge I'd spit it back again.'

Now guess who wishes he'd never asked that question! And talking of coffee being served, is it only me, or does everybody else who flies get the same treatment? As sure as night follows day, whenever the flight attendant serves me a cup of the dark stuff, the seat belt light comes on and we hit gale-force turbulence. Usually that results in having warmish fluid (never hot is it?) splashed all over you. Still I suppose that's chickenfeed compared to other people's miseries. For years Pat and I have sneaked off quietly for weekends in Paris and we still get a thrill from eating outdoors, sailing the Seine on the *bateaux mouches* and going to see shows. Generally speaking, we would attend two or three, but if time forbids, I always make for the Crazy Horse. The cabaret with the multi-lingual entertainers, the finest of dancers, the most stunning of speciality acts has to be seen to be believed. But the most incredible sight of all over the last few years has been the audiences. More and more folk from Japan and the eastern countries are touring Europe. Bless their hearts, they usually find themselves on a package, a hundred-mile-an-hour schedule – you know the type, twenty countries in forty minutes? By the time these lovely people arrive for an eight o'clock meal and cabaret, covered in cameras and camcorders, they are totally shattered. Our favourite pastime now is to count the number who gradually slump in their seats and let their heads sink slowly to the table in a peaceful slumber – little realizing that they are face down in bowls of soup.

Still, that's the glory of travel isn't it? Seeing exotic locations, eating exotic food and being totally exhausted and ill at the end of it all. Nothing really is ever what you expect it to be, and ignorance sometimes lends enchantment to the view. When I was young I used to make a habit of walking past Joe Lyons (does anyone remember them?) and breathing in that wonderful coffee aroma so special to those cafés. Never though, never in all my days, could I find a coffee that actually *tasted* the way it smelt. Years of research and whole cartons of coffee later my task was in vain until we stopped in South America on a cruise liner. In the city of Caracas, down a very quiet, rather dodgy-looking back street, we came across a tiny coffee house, full of wild-eyed locals and exuding that Joe Lyons perfume. In broken Spanish and charade-type gestures, I managed to explain that we would like the coffee that gave off that beautiful smell. Two cups were served by the owner, a man of few teeth, but all of different colours. One sip of this brew was enough for me. Here it was, after all those years. The nectar, the ambrosia, the Holy Grail of the drinks industry. Here at last was coffee that *tasted* like the smell I remembered. I think I had four cups, while trying to buy from the proprietor the beans or granules or whatever it was that he used to create this potion. All to no avail. 'No comprendi,' was his stock answer, and Pat and I left in search of food stores which might sell it. No luck, no joy. Sadly, truly sadly, we made our way back aboard and were greeted by the port lecturer, the person who knows all about the various places the ships visit. We explained our plight and wondered if he knew how to find the magical powder we sought.

'You won't like this,' he smiled, 'but as you look in fairly good shape I think I can explain the mystery to you. When we get coffee in supermarkets, the product has been totally refined, purified, granulated and what have you. When Mr Back Street coffee bar in Caracas gets it, it's still in the condition in which it was harvested. The beans are shovelled into sacks, along with anything else that's on the floor of the shed and it is delivered as is to the various outlets. Probably what gave your brew such a full-bodied taste was the dead beetles that had been ground in with the beans.'

I didn't speak for a full thirty seconds. I waited for his eyes to twinkle with laughter, but they didn't. So I nodded and turned on my heel. Now either this man is a latter-day Laurence Olivier, or my stomach has genuinely been through a very traumatic experience. Either way it's got me thinking that whenever we speak of diets, we naturally see pictures of food in various amounts. We give little thought to liquid sustenance and really we should. Depending on what we drink we can become healthy, wealthy, wise or just a gibbering wreck in need of Alka Seltzer.

That's All
– I Hope It's Enough

So here we are. The final chapter of our look at the idiosyncrasies of people who eat, drink, diet, carouse, and generally behave like normal people do. Because, be honest, nobody does more abnormal things than the normal person. I think we've all experienced the funny, peculiar and almost inexplicable happenings that surround us in everyday life. From the fireside to the great outdoors, it's surprising what humans get up to. But let's remember that in the general classification 'humans' we have to include ourselves.

Along with the weather, food and drink seem to make up ninety per cent of any conversation don't they? And so it has been throughout history. Take the Old Testament and the story of Solomon the wise one. Overheard in his court was the conversation between two ministers:

'They say he now has a hundred wives. I wonder how he feeds them?' said one.

'Never mind them,' replied the other. 'If he has a hundred happy wives, what does *he* eat?'

Moving on to medieval times, we know for a fact that, in order to punish thieves and the like, stocks were erected. The miscreants were locked in, and old fruit and vegetables were hurled in their direction. For some reason, that gave the more honest folk a feeling of well-being and satisfaction, a bit like banging the top of a television set when it's acting up. Of course, the stocks syndrome can be brought right up to date with the story of the music hall comedian who was on stage dying a death.

During the course of his not-too-funny routine he was aware of a heckler-type voice from the balcony. In reality, it was a man with a tray purveying fruit and veg to the audience.

'Our dog doesn't eat meat. Why? Because we don't give it any,' said the comic.

'Here we are, apples, oranges, ripe tomatoes,' came the voice on the balcony.

'My wife's gone to the West Indies. Jamaica? No, she went of her own accord,' ploughed on the act.

'Here we are, apples, oranges, ripe tomatoes,' persisted the vendor.

'I don't want London Bridge any longer. Why? It's long enough already,' persisted the turn.

'Here we are, apples, oranges. Apples, oranges,' came the voice.

'Oi,' bellowed the comedian, 'what happened to the ripe tomatoes?'

'Here they come now,' said the man on the balcony as the poor old entertainer was plastered.

Funny to imagine I suppose and maybe a ring of truth. It's even possible that the comedian involved may later have recounted it as part of an after-dinner speech, or even in an autobiography. I know I used many self-knocking stories in mine. It just seems that we mortals are possessed of a certain resilience gene that makes us see good even in the face of the worst evil.

Take the cartoon that made me smile. It featured two missionaries in a cannibal's pot, surrounded by bubbling water and gently boiling vegetables. As they peered out at the assembled tribesmen one said, 'Look, Carruthers, we've done it. They're saying grace.'

Ah yes, you can't beat a good cannibal cartoon. Or even a good cannibal recipe: 'To make an individual meat pie – first take one individual.'

But back to the 'corblimey' for a moment and let's look at things more domestic. An old farmer once told me that the most useful of all animals was the pig. I found that quite amazing when you compare the work of such beasts as horses, cows, oxen, chickens and such.

'Ah yes,' said he, 'but look how little it takes to house and feed the pig. Lives in muck, enjoys it, never complains and when it's dead you can eat all of it from snout to tail. In fact, the only thing you can't eat is the squeal.'

With this in mind it's almost possible to believe the story told to me by one of my heroes – Glen Campbell, the Country Singer. According to Glen, he was visiting a farmer friend in Kentucky and he noticed a pig wandering round the farmyard with what looked like a splint on its rear portions.

'What's that?' he asked.

'Ah that,' explained the farmer 'is a wooden leg.'

'A what?' said an amazed Glen.

'A wooden leg,' went on his pal. 'Only, you see times have been hard lately and the next meal has always been difficult to find. My wife suggested we kill and eat old porky, but he's been so dear to me over the years that I didn't have the heart to kill him, so we're eating him bit by bit.'

Thanks Glen, not a bad gag actually. Well, nobody would really do that, would they? Still, it's nice to squeeze out any fun there can be in a predicament. Like the news report supposedly broadcast on a local radio that stated,

'A thief broke into the delivery yard of a well-known grocery chain and drove off with a lorry-load of prunes. It happened late last night and he's been on the run ever since.'

Amazing what people do say, isn't it? Even in the most serious and even life-threatening moments there's that one, all too human, line that turns the reality into absurdity. Remember the epic case of the condemned man, in the days of capital punishment, who was roused from his cell by the executioner:

'Come on. It's time to meet your maker, lad.'

'But I'm not ready. For a start I haven't had my breakfast,' pleaded the prisoner.

'I don't know about your breakfast son,' apologized the headsman, 'I'm only here to see you don't get any dinner.'

And from a shortish expectancy of life to a much longer one. We must look to the children of the world. Those very special people who hold the future in their hands and a special place in our hearts. And while all youngsters are very special people, none is more so than our own. It's only natural really that we place family ties above all else, particularly at a time of stress. Like, for instance, a birthday party attended by seemingly endless legions of other people's offspring.

'Listen everybody,' screamed an almost totally distraught hostess, 'there is a very special prize for any

child who goes home right now!'

You know just how she feels don't you? But then these things happen at every gathering of children.

'Can I have some more cake?' asked little Peter of the lady of the house.

'Why Peter,' she said, 'didn't your mummy tell you never to ask for more?'

'Yes,' replied Peter, 'but she didn't realize how small the helpings were going to be.'

Another little lad, over excited and eating his way to happiness, was just about to tuck into a large slice of rhubarb tart when accosted by an adult.

'Johnny,' she cautioned, 'if you eat any more you'll burst.'

'All right,' said he, 'give me another slice and stand back.'

Sensible reasoning I suppose, if you're only five. Ah yes, the wisdom of youth, the logic of youth, so much less complicated than that of the adult world. Take the case of the youngster attempting a crossword puzzle in a magazine. The clue read 'four letters – to egg on'. The boy had no hesitation in writing 'Tost', ignoring the 'a' and ignoring the urge to discover 'urge' was what was required. When you're young if it fits and appears to work that's an end to the matter.

Funny that, how sometimes we grown-ups look too deeply into things when we should perhaps just go with the flow. For surely when ignorance is bliss it is folly to be wise, or even to challenge. Do you recall the classic tale of the man newly incarcerated in hospital and unused to hospital matters, who was busy trying to explain the happenings in his new abode?

'And do you know,' he said to a visiting workmate, 'the bloke in the bed opposite had a kidney removed yesterday. And on today's lunch menu they've got kidney soup. I tell you what pal, they waste nothing here.'

Take humans and victuals and you always get a comic combination. From Bible times when we have quotes such as:

'The Lord said to Moses come forth and he came fifth and got no pudding.'

On to today and the hot-from-the-presses type commercial jingles that inspire reaction:

'Charlie saw a sign saying "Drink Canada Dry" and we haven't seen him since.'

Wherever and whatever and whyever it seems that you cannot separate food and drink from fun and laughter. And, more, there always appear to be new ways in which the poor humble human can be dragged into the line of fire.

When I was a nipper in Liverpool, I learned of people's odd ways with grub and beverage. Take the docker's breakfast:

'A Woodbine, an aspirin and a good cough – guaranteed to start the heart on a cold winter's morn.'

Of course those were the days when smoking and drinking weren't harmful to you, or so the experts said. Although they were always a little sceptical of the alcoholic side of things. When confronted with a real heavy drinker, even the old outlook balked at encouragement. Take examples like my Aunt Lucy's husband Eric.

'What a drinker,' she used to moan, 'he'll drink anything with a kick in it – gin and aftershave – anything. The other day he said he'd always longed for the perfect stiff drink so I put starch in his whisky.'

It was Lucy who came out with that extremely wise piece of advice.

'Never give coffee to a boozer, you'll just end up with

a wide-awake drunk.'

And on the subject of wide awakedness (if there is such a word), what about the chap who had terrible trouble getting up for work in the mornings. Sure we have all been guilty of the odd lie-in I know, and there's always the temptation on a very cold morning to lie there and feign illness.

'I don't think I'll go in today, luv,' mumbled one over-comfortable soul. 'I'm not feeling too good and anyway it's foggy outside.'

'I know,' said his understanding wife, 'but it's not foggy over the roofs.'

'Yes,' he replied tetchily, 'but I wasn't thinking of going that way.'

But back to the point. We have a poor, unfortunate, unwakeable soul whose job is on the line if he comes in late once more.

'Do you know what you should do?' suggested a workmate. 'Keep off the booze and drink a nourishing nightcap. Try Horlicks, the food drink of the night. It'll help you to relax, get a good night's sleep and rise early, alert, alive and refreshed.' I tell you what, that's some advertising slogan in the making, isn't it?

So that night, our hero duly relaxed with the famous brand brew. Next day, he bounded into work as if on springs.

'What about this?' he smiled at his boss. 'It's only 8.30 am and here I am. Half an hour early, bouncing with energy and raring to go. What about this?'

'Yes,' sighed his boss, 'it's great, but where were you yesterday?'

Let's draw a veil over the outcome of that confrontation and try to sum up how we feel about the whole matter of staying alive. The basic rule harks back to that old music hall song, 'A little of what you fancy does you good.' An adage that's true of all features of human behaviour, particularly so when applied to caring for the most important part of our world – our mind and body. While it's nice from time to time to 'pig out' on rich and even exotic foods and drinks, the basic rule is to stick to reasonable portions of all things and never, as my grandmother used to say, 'Never leave the table either full or fasting.'

Let's be honest with ourselves. Unless we intend competing in the Olympics or Commonwealth Games, there's no great need to be super fit and sleek of form. Conversely, if we are to maintain a healthy and busy-ish way of life then we shouldn't be overblown caricatures of our normal selves. And, again conversely, unless we wish to tread the catwalks as the latest waif model, there is certainly no need to watch every calorie we consume or expend.

No, the world's a great place to be in and it's even greater when we have a positive attitude to it. And as in all things, the more we put into a day in the world the more we will eventually get out of it. So let's eat, drink and be merry and to heck with the Jonahs and the miseries. Live life to the full and remember that it is not a dress rehearsal – it's very much the real thing. Know your failings – mine's chocolate and biscuits, and be sure to monitor your indulgence. Know your strengths – mine is of will, forcing mind to eventually overpower matter. Although I must admit that while staring at a semi-fit image of myself in a mirror, I can't quite shake off the craving for chocolate fudge cake and ice-cream. Still, it makes that delicacy all the more wonderful to taste when I eventually drop my guard for a day-off treat.

So look. Be honest with yourself. You know the rights and wrongs in your make up. You know whether to

JIM HUTCHINGS

lose or gain weight. You know whether you are getting enough exercise or not. It matters not what I or any nutritional expert says – you and you alone are the master of your body and your fate. You and you alone can determine whether to enjoy every possible minute of your life. So be the boss, listen to your heart and do the right things. Not for me, but for yourself, determine to give life a go, smell the flowers, enjoy the restraints you place on yourself and you'll be surprised at the different you that you'll find.

So eat like a horse, drink like a fish but remember that of these creatures you've never seen a fat one or a skinny one.